LANDMARKS OF WORLD LITERATURE – SECOND EDITIONS

AESCHYLUS

The Oresteia

SIMON GOLDHILL

Professor of Greek, University of Cambridge,
and Fellow of King's College

CAMBRIDGE
UNIVERSITY PRESS

PUBLISHED BY THE PRESS SYNDICATE OF THE UNIVERSITY OF CAMBRIDGE
The Pitt Building, Trumpington Street, Cambridge, United Kingdom

CAMBRIDGE UNIVERSITY PRESS
The Edinburgh Building, Cambridge, CB2 2RU, UK
40 West 20th Street, New York, NY 10011–4211, USA
477 Williamstown Road, Port Melbourne, VIC 3207, Australia
Ruiz de Alarcón 13, 28014 Madrid, Spain
Dock House, The Waterfront, Cape Town 8001, South Africa
http://www.cambridge.org

First published 1992, second edition 2004

Printed in the United Kingdom at the University Press, Cambridge

Typeface Photina 10/12 pt.   *System* LATEX 2_ε [TB]

A catalogue record for this book is available from the British Library

ISBN 0 521 83229 2 hardback
ISBN 0 521 53981 1 paperback

Contents

Preface

There could be few works more suitable for the Landmark series than Aeschylus' trilogy, the *Oresteia*. It was a landmark from its first performance, recognized as the greatest work of a playwright who was recognized as the figurehead of the flourishing of tragedy in classical Athens. He still is. The *Oresteia* was, first of all, for the Greeks themselves, simply the most influential play ever written. Its dramatic techniques, narrative development and dense poetry changed the course of Greek and hence European drama. It is the play to which Euripides and Sophocles, the other great surviving playwrights of the fifth century, turned again and again in homage, competition and imitation. From here comes Western theatre.

What is more, particularly since the Romantic period, the *Oresteia* has had a continuing and powerful influence on European cultural production. It is the work Wagner struggled to mirror in the *Ring*; for Marx and Engels it is a central text in the development of their ideas on the family, private property and the state; T. S. Eliot, Sartre, O'Neill offer versions; Nietzsche and Hegel take it as a central example in their writings; from Kate Millett through to Hélène Cixous it has proved an important text for feminist cultural politics. With startling new performances in Paris, Berlin and London in recent years, the play has provoked new audiences to debate. The *Oresteia* is not a preserved monument, but the site of a continuing and profound engagement.

Yet the *Oresteia* is not easy to read. It was written first for Athens in 458 B.C. and this distance – of time and culture – provides a major barrier to the reader. The play was produced under quite different theatrical, political and social conditions from any modern drama. Not only have we lost the music, movements and stagings integral to the performance – none can be reconstructed with any certainty, though there are many attempts – but also we cannot assume that modern cultural expectations of theatrical experience will be less than grossly distorting for ancient theatre. The play was first staged on one day only in a state festival in honour of a god, Dionysus, a festival attended by what was said to be the whole city – namely, in the main, adult, enfranchised males. The city, Athens, was in the process of developing the first and in many ways most radical democratic system, and the performance of tragedy is part of that political process as we will see. The first chapter of this book, then, will look at the different contexts of Athenian tragedy to explore ways in which ancient culture and its categories provide particular conditions of production for the *Oresteia*.

Yet even within these contexts the play is not easy to read because of its intricate narrative patterns and dense lyric poetry. In the second chapter, I will develop some routes through the narrative of the trilogy, including some detailed analyses of passages of the play to demonstrate the complexity of Aeschylean Greek. Together, it is hoped, these discussions will enable the modern reader to take some first steps towards seeing why the *Oresteia* has proved itself one of the most remarkable works ever composed for the theatre.

Chronology

	Aeschylus' life and works	Historical and cultural events at Athens
528/7		Hippias the tyrant succeeded Peisistratus
525/4	Born at Eleusis	
507		Cleisthenes' reforms introduced democracy
?499	First dramatic production	Ionian revolt against Persian empire in Eastern Mediterranean
490	Fought at Marathon, where his brother, Cynegeiros was killed	Persians invade Greece. Athenians defeated Persians at Marathon
484	First victory in tragic competition	
483		Themistocles persuaded Athenians to build a huge fleet
480	Perhaps fought at Salamis	Xerxes, king of Persia, invaded Greece. Battles at Thermopylae, Artemisium, Salamis. Athens sacked
479		Greeks finally defeated Persians
478		Athens founded Delian League
?476	Visited Sicily to produce plays for Hieron, tyrant of Syracuse	
472	Won first prize with trilogy including *The Persians*; production financed by Pericles	

Chronology (cont.)

	Aeschylus' life and works	Historical and cultural events at Athens
470	Returned to Sicily; produced *Persians* there	Revolt of Naxos from Delian League. Harsh terms imposed by Athens
468		Sophocles' first prize in tragic competition
467	Won first prize with trilogy including *The Seven Against Thebes*	
?463	Won first prize with trilogy including *The Suppliant Maidens*	
462		Ephialtes' reforms
461		Ephialtes' assassination. Exile of Cimon
460		Athenian expedition to Egypt
458	Won first prize (18th and last time) with *The Oresteia*	
456	Died at Gela in Sicily	
455		Euripides' first play
454		Treasury of Delian League moved to Athens
451		Pericles' citizenship law
447		Parthenon started
431		Peloponnesian War started
429		Death of Pericles
404		Athens' defeat in Peloponnesian War

Chapter 1

Drama and the city of Athens

To exist outside a *polis* is to be either greater or less than human.
Aristotle

All our surviving tragedies were written for and performed first in one place, Athens, in the fifth century B.C. To understand tragedy, something of its cultural and historical frame must be appreciated. In this chapter, I consider four fundamental contexts for the genre of tragedy.

1 The context of the polis

Let us start, then, with a necessary word of Greek: *polis* (plural *poleis*). I must transliterate this because no translation – certainly not the usual translations 'city' or 'city-state' – captures the complex range of political, spatial, religious, historical and social ideas evoked by the Greek term. That I just used the modern term 'political', which is derived from the Greek term 'things to do with the *polis*', shows the problem neatly. For many modern readers, I expect, the term 'political' will imply a more or less narrow concern with government and institutions and ideological programmes – as in 'keep politics out of sport'. The *polis* in Greece, however, is the very condition of human existence (as the epigraph to this chapter claims) and 'things to do with the *polis*' – the political – embrace all aspects of a citizen's life. (Thus 'the personal is political' could have no purchase as a slogan in the fifth century, any more than could the claim that athletic achievement was not integrally linked to the standing of the citizen and his *polis*.) As Aristotle famously writes, 'Man is a political animal' – by which he means 'man necessarily and naturally lives in a *polis*'. Greek tragedy is both part of this life of the *polis* and repeatedly reflects on its audience's existence as 'political animals'. So it is first the crucial frame of the *polis* that I want to discuss.

1

My discussion will focus inevitably on Athens, in some ways a highly atypical *polis*, but I shall try in this first section of the chapter to show some ways in which Athens exemplifies certain common fifth-century ideas of the *polis*. I will begin, however, with some very general remarks about the fifth century as a specific period in the history of the *polis*.

Now the fifth century throughout Greece was a period of rapid and intense political change. The many different and largely autonomous communities that had grown up through the previous centuries faced similar pressures on three fronts. First, for a nexus of economic and social reasons, many *poleis* were racked by internal tensions particularly between a wealthy land-owning élite and the wider population. Ancient commentators describe a series of violent shifts of constitution – between oligarchy (rule by a few), tyranny (rule by one man) and democracy (rule by the many). So towards the end of the sixth century Athens was ruled by Peisistratus, a tyrant, who was succeeded by his son Hippias, but in 507, after many years of division, the reforms of Cleisthenes instituted the first democratic system, which provided Athens with its method of government for most of the fifth century and which I will discuss in the next section of this chapter. What is perhaps most remarkable, however, is not merely the violent political upheavals of this period, but the fact that they were accompanied by an intense, public and sophisticated debate about the processes and principles of change as they were taking place. This competitive self-scrutiny and self-criticism has been convincingly seen as a determining factor in what is known as the fifth-century enlightenment – that extraordinary burgeoning of arts, science, medicine and philosophy in the fifth century, centred on Athens (Lloyd 1987). Indeed, the institution of tragedy, and the *Oresteia* in particular, as we will see, can be viewed first as part of this continuing public debate on internal political developments.

The second major pressure on the *polis* comes from the East. From the beginning of the fifth century, Greek cities, particularly at first the Ionian cities of Asia Minor, were locked in a struggle with the Persian empire. Twice full-scale invasions of Greece were beaten off, notably at Marathon in 490, where the Athenians played a leading role and Aeschylus himself fought; and in 480/479, in a series of battles of which the sea battle at Salamis and the land battle at Plataia proved decisive. Aeschylus may have fought at Salamis too, and the *Persians*, his first surviving tragedy, dramatizes the expedition and the battle at sea from the point of view of the defeated Persians. The wars against Persia brought a heightened – and much debated – sense of 'Greekness' (as opposed to 'the barbarians') and led to active political debates on foreign policy and freedom. The *Oresteia*, like many tragedies, has as its background the war of the Greeks against the Trojans (the 'barbarian' East) and ends with the *polis* of Athens being exhorted to victory in conflicts away from Athens itself. Here, too, then, tragedy takes place against the significant political backdrop of major conflict.

The third pressure – partly a result of the defeat of Persia – was the rise and conflict of Athenian and Spartan imperialism in the Greek world. Themistocles had persuaded the Athenians to invest the income from the newly discovered silver mines at Laureion in a huge fleet (instrumental in the victory at Salamis). After the threat from Persia diminished, Athens was a driving force in the formation of the 'Delian League', a group of allies formed for mutual defence and reparations against Persia. Athens rapidly assumed hegemony, and, in 454, four years after the *Oresteia*, transferred the treasury of the League from the island of Delos to the Acropolis in Athens. Here Pericles persuaded the Assembly to use the funds both to adorn Athens – the Parthenon is the most famous result of this programme – and, more importantly, to finance an increasingly imperialist campaign throughout the Mediterranean (as 'allies' became more and more tribute states under Athens' domination). This brought Athens into conflict with Sparta and throughout the latter part of the fifth century Athens and Sparta were in conflict – the Peloponnesian War. Our surviving tragedies are co-extensive with the spread – and fall – of the Athenian empire, which had an effect throughout the Greek world.

Much of the fifth century, then, was dominated by internal division and external conflict both between *poleis* and between Greece and her neighbours. The internal strife of the *polis*, however, focused not merely on who should hold the offices of government but also on the category of 'citizen' (*polites*). Citizenship implies belonging, being an insider, and there was an acute difference in privilege, status and position between citizens and non-citizens. Legal definitions of citizenship were increasingly debated – we know of several fourth-century law-cases contesting the issue from Athens – but being a citizen also implied a much wider set of ideas, all of which start from a criterion of being male, adult and Greek. (As Socrates is said to have pronounced, with a characteristically Greek sense of polarity, 'I thank god I was born a human and not an animal, a man and not a woman, a Greek and not a barbarian.') So, in Athens, only adult males could be citizens (women were not even known as 'Athenians' but as 'women of Attica'); and Pericles in 451 instigated a law which made it a requirement for citizenship that one's father should be a citizen and one's mother the daughter of a citizen. This not only restricted eligibility for citizenship drastically, but also effectively outlawed marriage between people of different *poleis* (thus destroying the traditional links by marriage between aristocratic families across Greece). The distinction between citizen and non-citizen was especially important in Athens, where, as the major commercial and cultural centre of Greece, there was an exceptionally large population of resident aliens ('metics') as well as slaves.

Citizenship implied first and foremost a duty and obligation to the *polis*. That a man should act to benefit his *polis* and that a *polis* benefited from a man's individual success are repeatedly asserted ideals. That a man should be prepared to fight and die for his *polis* is a given. That the community of the *polis* is the necessary foundation for religious, commercial and social life is largely taken for granted. Indeed, this ideology of *commitment to the polis* is so pervasive and strong that it remains a standard explanation of behaviour even (or especially) throughout the rebellions and civil discord of the fifth century. To be a citizen (*polites*), then, is to be in all senses a man of the *polis*.

In the light of this integral connection of citizenship, birth and the city, it is not surprising that there is a close connection between the *polis* and its land (Osborne). Even Athens, one of the largest communities, remained primarily an agricultural community where even the furthest territory was within at least an extended walking distance of the urban centre (approximately 70 kilometres). The *polis* often owned central areas, particularly of religious or military significance, and almost no property market developed in Greece. To move to another city thus meant either becoming a resident alien of greatly restricted rights or being forced into exile. Being a citizen implied an integral relation with the land of the *polis* – the fatherland.

Much religious life was focused on the *polis* too, with its temples, communal sacrifices and its festivals (Athens claimed it had more festivals than any other *polis*) (Easterling and Muir). The architecture, the religious ceremonies, the myths not only helped form the community of the *polis* as a community through shared activities and space, but also reflected and helped transmit and reinforce communal values (Vernant 1980; Gordon; Vernant 1983; Vidal-Naquet). It is not by chance, for example, that the Parthenon represents in its sculptures the community of Athens in worship and juxtaposes that image to two mythological subjects. First, the Amazons – wild women – being defeated in battle by Theseus, the king of Athens, who first organized Athens as a *polis*; and secondly, centaurs – monstrous half-men, half-beasts – in conflict with the civilized, human Lapiths. The civilized world of Athens and its values are surrounded, framed and defined by the defeat of figures who represent different forms of wildness, different forms of transgression (Tyrrell). As the Amazons became increasingly associated (particularly in such iconography) with the barbarian East, the representations of the victory of civilized Athens further enforce the significant connections between religious and political aspects of the *polis*.

So, too, being a citizen implied a (shared) history of the *polis*. For the Athenians, the defeat of the Persians at Marathon rapidly became a story of self-definition where the few, hardy, well-trained, disciplined Greeks defeated the soft, undisciplined, wealthy multitudes of the East. So, too, the foundation of a city is telling in the expression of citizenship: Athenians recounted how the first inhabitants of Attica sprang from the soil itself. Not only were women thus bypassed in a myth of origin – and women, as we have seen, could not be citizens in Athens – but also the integral connection of citizen to the land of the *polis* here receives a 'charter myth', which tells how the citizen is in all senses 'of the land'. The community of citizens defines itself partly through a shared myth of the past of the *polis*.

The *polis* inevitably provides the focus of social life also. The market place – *agorá* – is the central site of exchange – of goods, money, gossip, religion. It is a place where times of leisure for the adult male could regularly be spent. The gymnasium became a potent symbol of Greek culture for other cultures around the Mediterranean: it is where the citizens met to exercise naked (a thoroughly unoriental notion), to compete (in status, not merely in sport) and to form alliances – social and erotic. It is another public space of the *polis*. The sense of community and involvement implied by my phrase 'commitment to the *polis*' spreads throughout the fabric of fifth-century society.

To sum up so far, for the fifth-century Greek it was generally speaking an accepted principle that 'the good life was possible only in a *polis*, that the good man was more or less synonymous with the good citizen, that slaves, women and barbarians were inferior by nature and so excluded from all discussion' (Finley). Yet one qualification is immediately necessary, and to make it I need to add another Greek word to the discussion, namely, *oikos*. The *oikos*, which is often translated 'household', implies the physical house, the idea of home, the household members (alive and dead, slave and free); it indicates land, crops, chattels. A repeatedly expressed ideal of the *oikos* is its continuity: economic continuity in financial security; generational continuity in the production of legitimate sons; spatial continuity in that it exists across time in one place (hence the lack of a property market that I mentioned earlier). This ideal of the continuity of the *oikos* is one of the most lasting and binding norms of Greek cultural life. The *oikos* is the site of the private life of the citizen, and, as we will see, the more the ideology of the commitment of the citizen to the *polis* develops, particularly in the radical democracy of Athens, the more the ideals of the *polis* and the ideals of the *oikos* can be perceived to be in conflict. The *Oresteia* which starts in the home of one family and moves to the law-court of the city traverses the tensions produced by these two sites of authority in fifth-century culture, the *oikos* and the *polis*.

It will be evident that in my discussion so far I have followed in broad outline the modern categories that I mentioned in my opening paragraph – political, spatial, religious, historical, social. In part, my aim has been to show how what might appear to be natural modern distinctions inevitably overlap and interrelate in the idea of the *polis*. So, for example, the myth of birth from the soil that I mentioned constructs a narrative that bears on the religious sense of the city, its history, its sense of place, its sense of citizenship and the social implications of such a narrative of power and gender. It is – to put it more neatly – a tale of and for the *polis*.

2 *The context of democracy*

Athens, however, was no ordinary *polis*. Not only was it particularly large in population, territory and ambition, but also its radical democracy affected all aspects of its culture throughout the fifth century, and it is now to the specific context of democracy that I wish to turn.

This is not the place for a full history of democratic reform or for a full description of the institutions of democracy. Accounts are readily available for each period of Athenian history (Forrest; Manville; Sinclair; Ober; Hansen). But I will begin with some brief comments on the development and organization of Athenian democracy before turning to the way democracy and tragedy interrelate.

Although democracy emerged slowly, painfully and with many changes of policy and institution, the reforms of Cleisthenes constitute a major turning point. It is difficult to know precisely the range of local institutions – e.g. villages, kinship groups, religious organizations – that Cleisthenes faced, but what is clear is that he completely reorganized the sociopolitical structure of Attica. First he drew up boundaries for and organized citizens' affiliations to demes (139 or 140 of them, later rising to 174). Demes were local organizations, based on territorial and thus inevitably also on kinship ties. Enrolment on the register of the deme became a necessary criterion for citizenship. Local politics and other aspects of cultural life were organized through the demes. Indeed, from this time onwards, the name of a citizen's deme became the standard way of referring to a man, along with his father's name. (So, for example, Aeschylus' full name was *Aiskhulos Euphorionos Eleusinieus*, 'Aeschylus, son of Euphorion, of the deme Eleusis'.) The deme thus rapidly became and remained a fundamental unit of the social fabric of Athens.

Cleisthenes also established ten tribes. Each deme was assigned to a tribe; and each tribe was deliberately constructed to be roughly equal in size and to have demes from three different areas of Attica, the city itself, the sea-board and the inland territories. The tribes were thus designed to widen affiliation and to reduce conflict between different areas of the territory of Attica.

The main decision-making and legislative body was the Assembly, which every citizen had the right to attend. It voted on all policies (one citizen, one vote) after a debate. Each debate was introduced by the famous formula 'Who wishes to speak?', a formulation which implied that every citizen, regardless of wealth, birth or position had an equal right to address the people – a very cornerstone of democratic principle (even if in practice some citizens proved more equal than others . . .). The business of the Assembly was prepared by a Council of 500 citizens over the age of thirty who were elected each year, as were most officials in Athens, by lot. The position was not renewable (it could only be held twice and not in consecutive years); there was a compulsory geographical spread of councillors; all officials had to present full accounts at the end of their year of office. The Council was also charged with putting into action the will of the Assembly, and the balance between the executive Council and policy-making Assembly was essential to the practice of democracy.

The institutions of law are also fundamental to democracy. From the time of Ephialtes' reforms in 462, most court cases in what was a highly litigious society were held before popular courts where jurors were chosen by lot from a roster of 6,000 volunteers and paid by the state. Equality of all citizens before the law and the binding authority of the laws of the city were central tenets of democratic ideology. This ideal is enacted most famously by Socrates who, when convicted, elected to stay in prison and be executed rather than flee to exile and safety, but thus transgress the laws' authority. Democracy, with its publicized laws, enacted by consent in public by the public, significantly depicted itself as the polar opposite of tyranny, the unaccountable rule by force of one man. Democracy and the openness of the legal process were thus constructed as mutually implicative and mutually authorizing.

Although one should not underestimate the difficulty poorer citizens or those from outlying territory would have faced in taking full part in the apparatus of government, considerable participation of an extended range of citizens was necessary for the running of the

polis (Sinclair; Hansen; Ober). Not only could such pressing matters as the declaration of war be discussed by the prospective soldiers and sailors; but also within a single decade, something between a quarter and a third of citizens could reasonably expect to have served on the Council, the executive body of government. With its lack of bureaucracy and hierarchy of office, its selection of officials by lot, and with its immediate involvement in the maintenance and application of law, this direct democracy is far removed from modern Western representative government. The 'commitment to the *polis*' that I described as a basic fifth-century ideological force finds its institutional pinnacle in Athenian democracy.

I mentioned above the standard assumption that a citizen should be prepared to fight and die for the *polis* (as indeed Aeschylus fought at Marathon and perhaps Salamis). It must never be forgotten to what degree Athens is a warrior society and how deeply militarism is linked to democracy throughout the fifth century. Athens had a largely citizen militia – to be a soldier or sailor for most of the century one had to be a citizen; to be a citizen carried an expectation of military activity for the *polis*. I have pointed out that a declaration of war was debated in the Assembly by the prospective soldiers: what is striking is that the Assembly voted themselves into war nearly every year of the fifth century and no two years in succession passed without a campaign. 'War is to a man what marriage is to a woman', writes Vernant of fifth-century Athens – by which he means war provides the institution through which a man becomes fully a man, standing in the battle-line with his fellow citizens (as marriage and childbirth are necessary criteria for the title 'woman'). In democratic Athens, warfare is another integral element of what it means to be a *polites*, a man of the *polis*.

It is particularly fascinating, then, to see how the 'commitment to the *polis*' combines with the obligations of a direct democratic system and with Athenian militarism to produce a collective military ideology that pervades the institutions, language and activities of Athenian democracy. One institution shows this with especial force, namely the collective burial of the war dead (Loraux). Burial in Greek society was traditionally a family affair. But in Athens from at least around the 470s those who had died fighting for the city received a collective burial, carried to the grave, tribe by tribe, on wagons.

The markers raised over the graves listed the bare names of those who had fallen and did not give the father's name or deme name, those usual markers of identification. The dead lay just as Athenian citizens. The whole population was allowed to attend the burial, and an orator chosen by the city addressed the people.

The most famous surviving example of such a Funeral Oration is Pericles' Funeral Speech as represented in the work of the historian Thucydides (II.35–46), and it is a speech that has been repeatedly used to demonstrate the public projection of the ideals of democratic ideology. Certainly when Pericles says of Athenian citizens that 'all of us are fit to judge . . . each of us is willing to fight and die', he resoundingly enforces the democratic rallying cries of Assembly, law-court, navy and army that I have been discussing. So too he proclaims that 'We give our obedience to those whom we put in positions of authority and we obey the laws themselves' and that 'when it is a question of settling private disputes, everyone is equal before the law', just as 'no-one, so long as he has it in him to be of service to the state, is kept in political obscurity because of poverty'. Indeed, the requirement of participation is such that 'we do not say that a man who takes no interest in the affairs of the *polis* minds his own business; we say he has no business here at all'. Pericles' speech thus praises the Athenian system as 'an education for all Greece', and goes on to contrast it at length with that of their enemies the Spartans. In Pericles' whole speech, however, no individual is mentioned; no individual feat of valour singled out. The speech praises the whole city as a collective, engaged in a collective enterprise: 'this, then, is the kind of city for which these men, who could not bear the thought of losing her, nobly fought and nobly died. It is only natural that everyone of us who survives them should be willing to undergo hardships in her service.' Both the institution of the collective burial of those who died fighting for the *polis* and the speech celebrating their burial thus project and promote the collective ideals of democratic Athens.

It is in Athenian democracy alone that tragedy develops in the fifth century. In the next section of this chapter I will look at ways in which the tragic festival is particularly related to democracy. But by way of conclusion for this section, I want briefly to look at one way in which the *Oresteia* is linked very closely to the history and practice of democracy. Four years before the first production of the *Oresteia*, a man named Ephialtes was the figurehead of a major reform of the democratic legal system. The Areopagus was an important court that was involved in many political issues, but its members were chosen only from those who had held the office of archon (which barred it to the lowest echelons of society). Although the archons were by now selected by lot, the Areopagus remained a bastion, or at least symbol, of traditional authority. Ephialtes succeeded in having all the powers of the Areopagus removed and devolved to the popular courts and to the Council, save the right to judge murder trials and certain religious crimes (such as damage to the sacred olive stumps). This change took place under the slogan of a return to the Areopagus' original and proper function. The effect of the reform was to decrease radically the power of the aristocrats and to increase the authority and jurisdiction of the popular courts. Ephialtes was assassinated shortly afterwards. (In return, Cimon, another leading political figure who had been to the fore in fighting the Persians, but who was a conservative in domestic politics, was exiled in the same year of turbulent political activity.) In the *Eumenides*, the third play of the *Oresteia*, Athene is depicted establishing the Areopagus – we see staged its 'charter myth' – and this court then tries Orestes for the murder of his mother. It is important that the *Oresteia* is the only surviving tragedy to have a scene thus set in the heart of Athens itself (albeit in the distant past). Athene makes a long speech about the Areopagus and its functions. Although critics have passionately disagreed about what this scene may indicate about Aeschylus' own political views, as we will see in section 15 of this book, one thing is clear. This scene of the play addresses in a direct way a central and highly controversial political event of the day, one fundamental to the organization of power within the *polis*. The *Oresteia*, then, is expressly engaging with the development of democracy in Athens, as it is directed towards the audience of the *polis* in the theatre.

3 The context of the festival

How does tragedy as a genre and the festival in which tragedy was performed relate to democracy? Is there a necessary link between democracy and tragedy?

The *Oresteia* was performed in a festival called the Great or City Dionysia. Although there was another less important festival, the Lenaia, at which drama was also performed from 440 B.C. in the city of Athens, and as the century advanced, performances of tragedy in particular spread further afield in Greece, it is primarily the Great Dionysia that provides the festival context for tragedy in Aeschylus' lifetime.

Let me begin with a brief description of the organization of the occasion itself. The chief official for the festival was the so-called Eponymous Archon (one of ten archons, or magistrates, appointed each year in fine democratic fashion by lot, one from each tribe from a list of five hundred candidates supplied by the demes). One of his first jobs on appointment was to select three poets to produce tragedies (and from 486, when comedy was introduced into the Great Dionysia, five comic playwrights). The playwrights were, to use the Greek phrase, 'granted a chorus'. We know nothing of the criteria used for choosing the poets. Then the Eponymous Archon appointed *choregoi*, prominent individuals whose duty it was to finance the performance of a poet's work by paying for the chorus. A similar system of financing – called the 'liturgy' system – was used for most festivals and for military expenditure too. The liturgy both acted as a tax on the wealthy and enabled the wealthy to compete for status with greater displays of largesse towards the city. Aeschylus was funded at least once in his career by Pericles, who became the most powerful and influential politician of the era. Actors too were assigned to plays by lot. There were three actors for each play, who divided the different roles between them – a procedure which required considerable virtuosity from the actors, who might be required to play a young girl and an old man in the same play. All the actors were male and were citizens. The Great Dionysia was, then, first and foremost a festival controlled, financed and organized by the democratic *polis*.

In the ninth month of the calendar year, roughly corresponding to our March, the festival took place. Before the festival proper started, the statue of Dionysus, the god in whose honour the festival took place, was removed from its precinct next to the theatre, taken out of the city, and brought in procession from the village of Eleutherai outside Athens to the theatre, where it stood throughout the festival. A couple of days before the plays, the playwrights publicly announced the subjects of their plays, and presented their casts to the city in a ceremony called the *proagon*. The first day of the festival proper began, however, as with so many religious occasions in Greece, with a huge procession (*pompe*), in this case of citizens, metics and others, all finely dressed, many carrying models of an erect phallus, a Dionysian symbol of fertility and celebration. Bulls were led too for a sacrifice that ended in a huge feast of meat (rarely eaten by Athenians, except on festival occasions) and wine. There were competitions of choral singing, with men's and boys' choruses, organized on a tribal basis (and funded by liturgies). Even prisoners on 'death-row' were released from custody on bail to join the communal celebrations.

On each of the next three days, each of the three tragic playwrights presented three tragedies and a satyr play. The three tragedies could be connected as in Aeschylus' *Oresteia*, but also could be on three separate topics, though it is unclear to what degree such plays might have been thematically linked. The satyr play always had a chorus of satyrs (half-men, half-goats with tails and constant erections) and were short, often uproarious, vulgar and escapist plays, that offered release from the tension of tragedy, as well as a thoroughly Dionysiac experience (the satyrs are the miscreant attendants of the god). Before the tragedies took place, a series of ceremonies were performed in the theatre (Goldhill 1990). There were first a sacrifice and a libation poured by the ten generals (the ten most important – and elected, rather than chosen by lot – military and political officials of the state). It was quite rare for the generals to act together in this way: no more than four such religious occasions are recorded in any one year, and this appears to be the only regular occasion in the calendar when all the generals perform such a ritual. Second, there was an announcement of the names of all those citizens who had benefited the *polis* and who had thus been awarded a crown (an honorific gesture by the state). This was an occasion publicly to emphasize the duties and obligations of the citizen to the *polis* (as well as praising prominent individuals). Third, there was a parade of young men, whose fathers had died fighting for the *polis*. These orphans were supported by the *polis* and educated at public expense, and when they reached the age of manhood they were paraded in full armour, again provided by the *polis*, and they publicly affirmed a proclamation that as their fathers had died for the *polis*, here they stood ready to take their places in the military ranks. Another opportunity is thus taken to demonstrate publicly the duties of the democratic citizen – duties conceived here precisely in terms of the military obligations I discussed briefly above. After 454, a fourth ceremonial also took place – the display of the tribute of the states of the Athenian empire, ingot by ingot of silver. It is not hard to see how this huge procession of allies' tribute glorified the military and political influence of Athens. The four ceremonials before the plays, then, use a state festival to project and promote the self-image of the state as military and political power, and to stage the binding affiliation of citizen to state. It is not only the plays but the whole occasion that addresses the citizen body. The Great Dionysia is in all senses truly a festival of the democratic *polis*.

On the fifth day of the festival, the five comedies were staged. (During the Peloponnesian War, it seems that only three comedies were performed, one after each of the tragedian's offerings. Thus, during the war the festival lasted only four days; though no explicit reasons for this cut-back survive, the war itself has been plausibly suggested to be a major factor, with the need to transfer funds to the military effort.) Two days later an Assembly was held in the theatre to consider how the festival had been conducted – the democratic requirement of accountability.

The tragedians with their *choregoi* were in competition: ten judges, one per tribe, were elected by lot in a complex procedure designed to avoid any chance of bribery or prejudice. The competition was fiercely and often passionately undertaken, and not merely by the writers and their funders. After 449, there was also a competition for actors in tragedies (and from 442 for actors in comedies too). That the production of plays was competitive is typical of Athenian culture. The Assembly, with competing proposals being put to the vote; the law-court with prosecutor and defendant judged by a large citizen audience; the gymnasium with its wrestling bouts, races and erotic pursuits (not to mention the Olympics and other pan-hellenic games) – all these are institutions for which competition is a fundamental structuring principle. Greek and especially

Athenian culture was at all levels highly competitive, despite the ideological projections of equality and communal commitment.

There are many ways, then, in which this *polis*-funded, *polis*-organized, *polis*-accountable festival is paradigmatic of Athenian democratic institutions. Yet there is a further and perhaps more important way that the Great Dionysia and its genres of drama are a product of democracy. For the plays themselves, as much as the festival, are deeply imbued with a spirit of competition. The *agon*, or formal debate/contest/ struggle, is a repeated and basic element of all Greek drama. Often character faces character, expresses a position with a set speech, is opposed by a set speech, and the scene turns to passionate line by line disagreement. This formal element – an analogue to the Assembly and law-court – is perhaps the key sign and symptom of what Vernant and Vidal-Naquet call 'the tragic moment'.

By 'the tragic moment' these influential French scholars are proposing an answer to the question of why did tragedy arise at this time and in this place. For them, tragedy as a genre appears at a particular moment of an unresolved clash between two general views of man's place in the world – which they call the 'archaic' and the 'legal'. The importance of law to democracy has been stressed already. The legal system assumes that a man is responsible for his actions, can be judged as a responsible individual for those actions, and that punishment is to be weighed out according to that judgement. In the mythical and heroic traditions of archaic society, however, it is the justice of the gods that prevails. So in Homer error, success, desire, even the flight of an arrow or the glance of a woman are directed by the immediate and explicit influence of divinities (and the whole *Iliad* is placed under the rubric of 'the plan of Zeus'). Tragedy takes place, then, at the moment of maximal unresolved tension between such systems of ideas – it is both sign and symptom of such tensions. As Vernant and Vidal-Naquet write: 'The tragic turning point thus occurs when a gap develops at the heart of social existence. It is wide enough for the opposition between legal and political thought on the one hand, and the mythical and heroic tradition, on the other, to stand out quite clearly. Yet it is narrow enough for the conflict in values to be a painful one and for the clash to continue to take place.' Tragedy thus stages through its structure of the *agon* a division in social thought. It explores the different and competing ideals, different and competing obligations, different and competing senses of words in the developing *polis*, different and competing ideas of glory and success. It shows characters failing to communicate, clinging to ideas, and tearing themselves and society apart. It discovers tensions and ambiguities within the very civic ideology of democracy that is the context of tragedy's performance.

The Greeks, as ever, have a word for it: *es meson*, which can literally be translated 'into the middle', but within fifth-century democracy means 'to be put into the public domain to be contested'. Tragedy takes the developing notions, vocabulary, commitments of democracy and places them under rigorous, polemical, violent and *public* scrutiny. Athenian democracy prided itself on the openness of its institutions and its willingness to have both sides of a case heard (however much practice could distort such ideology). None the less, this civic occasion on which a society gathered together to stage a sophisticated, searching, moving exploration of its own beliefs and processes remains – not least for our Western society – a remarkable and salutary example.

4 *The context of the theatre*

If the social and ideological background of theatre is so different from today, what of the theatrical resources themselves? We have seen how the festival context of Greek tragedy radically alters the sense of how theatre functions as a social experience. Now, to conclude this opening chapter, we must look briefly at the theatre itself.

I have already described how each playwright was required to compose three tragedies and a satyr play for the competition, and how the selection was termed 'to be granted a chorus'. The chorus remains one of the most difficult areas of Greek dramaturgy to appreciate and I wish to start my consideration of the theatre with it. The chorus was made up of citizens (so too, as I have mentioned, were the actors: there was no sub-class of 'theatricals' as in Rome, even when the actors formed guilds and famous acting families grew up through the fifth and fourth centuries). There were probably twelve members of the chorus of the *Oresteia*, though some scholars argue, perhaps rightly, that fifteen, the usual number in later years,

is likely for Aeschylus too (Taplin). The chorus' members were selected for a performance (like the actors) and were trained by a special trainer for the songs and dances they were required to perform.
Like the actors, the chorus was fully masked. These masks were not
the grotesque 'tragic masks' with down-turned mouths and gap-
ing eyes, familiar from modern theatre decorations, but carefully
painted figural representations. The chorus performed in a dancing area called the *orchestra*, below the raised stage on which the
actors performed. It became normal that there was a backdrop in
the form of a house/palace with a door, through which a trolley
could be rolled to reveal a prepared tableau (the *ekkuklema*), and it
has been plausibly suggested that the *Oresteia* is the first work we
have to use this later standard organization of stage space. Actors
entered through the door or from long entrance ways to the left and
right of the acting space. The acting space with its separate areas
thus helped create a specific dialectical relation between collective
chorus in the *orchestra* and individual actors on the stage.

Although modern stage conventions often find it hard to deal
with a constant collective presence on stage, the difficulties of inter-
preting the role of the chorus go beyond this difference of audience
expectation, and stem from what can be seen as a duality of role.
On the one hand, the chorus sings the choral odes that divide the
different scenes of the drama. These were accompanied by music
and dance (both these aspects of performance have been lost), and
these songs contain the drama's densest lyric poetry that often comments on and reacts to the previous scene of the play. These choral
odes often speak from a general and generalizing viewpoint. On the
other hand, the chorus also takes part in the scenes of the play as a
dramatic persona and engages from a specific point of view in the
scenic action.

Let us explore this duality a little further. The chorus as an institution is deeply embedded in Greek culture. To sing and dance in
choruses was a normal and basic part of education for both boys
and girls: it was a way of passing down the privileged narratives of
a culture in a collective and didactic form. So, too, as I have mentioned, there were other choral competitions at the Great Dionysia,
where the ten tribes provided five men's and five boys' choruses.
Thus it is easy to see why the chorus in tragedy is often treated as

the most expressly didactic voice of the play. Few today would say it expresses simply the views of the poet himself (as many Victorian critics liked to believe), but many would argue that the collective voice of the chorus mirrors, mediates and otherwise directs the collective response of the audience. A collective sounding-board, as it were, for the collective of the *polis*.

Yet the chorus is made up also of specific, even characterized figures, who speak from a particular perspective and with particular interests. How is the collective, generalizing, didactic voice of the chorus to be related to this sense of individual characterization? The problem is most acutely realized in the *Eumenides*, the third play of the *Oresteia*. The chorus of this play is made up of the Furies (*Erinyes*), who pursue Orestes to exact blood vengeance. They also sing a long ode about justice in the city. How are their general reflections on justice, then, to be related to their pursuit of blood vengeance? I do not think that there can be a single model which will explain – or predict – how generally or how specifically any particular chorus' remarks are to be taken. Rather, I would prefer to see the chorus' collective voice as posing for the audience a problem of relating common wisdom or general views to the specific incidents of the drama. I have described tragedy as provoking, exploring, questioning notions about the city's behaviour and ideals. The chorus as collective voice has a particular role to play in the *agon* of attitudes that makes up tragedy. It requires the audience to engage in a constant renegotiation of where the authoritative view lies. It sets in play an authoritative collective voice, but surrounds it with other dissenting voices. The chorus both allows a wider picture of the action to develop, and also remains one of the many views expressed. The chorus is thus a key dramatic device for setting in play commentary, reflection and an authoritative collective voice as part of tragic conflict.

What of the audience of the drama? The spectators – perhaps as many as 16,000 – were ranged in wedge-shaped sections in the amphitheatre. The front seats were reserved for dignitaries. It is also likely that the seating was arranged by tribal division, with each tribe seated in a particular wedge. The theatre thus mapped the city in its space as it addressed the city in its plays. Over the years, foreigners attended the Great Dionysia with increasing frequency, and, after the transfer of the treasury from Delos, the ambassadors who brought the tribute to Athens sat in the theatre to watch its display. Unfortunately, we do not have any decisive piece of evidence that can demonstrate whether women were allowed in the theatre. Scholars debate the issue at length, but without a consensus. One thing is clear, however: if there were any women there, they were in the vast minority and were not the 'proper or intended' audience (Henderson). Greek tragedy, with its all-male cast, all-male producers and writers and male audience, remains a citizen affair.

With masked male actors, a singing, dancing, masked male chorus, a vast audience seated according to the formal sociopolitical divisions of the state, in a five-day festival in honour of the god Dionysus, a festival whose ceremonies are replete with social and cultural significance . . . the contexts of Greek tragedy are far removed, indeed, from Western bourgeois theatre, tragedy's heir.

So, then, Greek tragedy should not be viewed simply as an aesthetic, emotional or ritual experience (although it is all three of these). It is also an event that places the tensions and ambiguities of a rapidly developing political and cultural system in the public domain to be contested. What is more, the *Oresteia* itself ends, unlike all other extant tragedies, in the centre of the democratic *polis* of Athens, its law-court. The play speaks to the *polis*. The *Oresteia* is in the full sense of the term a *political* drama; and awaits your – our – verdict.

Chapter 2

The *Oresteia*

5 *Introduction: plot and plotting*

The action of the *Oresteia* – in the sense of entrances, exits, deaths, adulteries and the like – is relatively simple to explain. What makes the trilogy so extraordinary is the intricate apparatus of explanation, comment and discussion with which its thrillingly dramatic central actions are surrounded.

In the *Agamemnon*, Agamemnon returns home, victorious from Troy after a ten-year siege, and he is killed by his wife, Clytemnestra, who has been plotting with her lover, Aegisthus. In the *Choephoroi*, Orestes, the son of Clytemnestra and Agamemnon, returns from exile, has a reunion with his sister, Electra, and tricks his way into the palace where he kills Aegisthus and his mother. He flees, maddened by the Furies. In the *Eumenides*, Orestes is in Delphi, where he is purified by Apollo; but he is still pursued to Athens by the Furies, where he is the subject of the first murder trial in the court of the Areopagus. The Furies prosecute, Apollo defends. Orestes escapes by the narrowest of margins, thanks to the intervention of Athene, who presides over the case. The Furies are persuaded out of their anger against Athens and, reconciled, take up abode there.

This bare outline of the action scarcely represents the narrative. In the *Agamemnon*, the return of the king is prepared for in two major ways. First, by three extremely long and complex choral odes that explore the moral, historical and social background to the war with Troy. Secondly, by three scenes. In the first, the prologue, a watchman laments the disorder of the house of Agamemnon and then sees the beacon light for which he has been set to wait. In the second, the queen Clytemnestra explains to a disbelieving chorus of city elders how the beacon has arrived from Troy and what it portends – the fall of Troy and the imminent return of Agememnon. In the third, a messenger arrives ahead of the king, with a verbal report of the sack of Troy and news of a storm that has wrecked the returning Greeks – though Agamemnon has landed safely.

The killing of the king also is dramatized in a protracted series of scenes. The entrance to the palace is blocked by Clytemnestra, who in a famous and brilliantly dramatic scene spreads blood-red tapestries in front of the door; the king, who initially refuses to trample such finery, is persuaded by Clytemnestra to enter his palace across the tapestries. Clytemnestra fails to persuade Cassandra, a Trojan princess, who is part of the king's booty, to come in immediately, and she is left on stage with the chorus. Cassandra is an inspired prophetess and she begins to describe in an extraordinarily intricate and powerful set of images both the past history of the family and its future violences. She eventually enters the house knowingly to her death. Then the death cries of Agamemnon are heard off-stage – and Clytemnestra appears over the bodies for another exchange of accusation and defence between the queen and chorus. Finally, Aegisthus enters to explain his motivation for the murder. And the queen and her lover are left in control of the house.

In the *Choephoroi*, there is a similar pattern of extended preparation for the central confrontation of protagonists, mother and son. First, Orestes returns with his companion Pylades to pray at the tomb of his father for divine support. Electra and the chorus of female palace servants enter, also on their way to the tomb, carrying libations from Clytemnestra (hence the play's title which means 'libation bearers', as it is sometimes called in translations of the trilogy). Clytemnestra has had a terrifying dream and has sent her daughter to appease the spirit of Agamemnon with the libations. Electra changes the words of the prayer, however, and pours libations in the hope of 'just vengeance'. She then spots Orestes' offerings and footprint and immediately leaps to the conclusion that her brother has returned; he reveals himself, and an ecstatic reunion leads first to Orestes' explanation of how Apollo has told him to come and seek vengeance for his father, and then to a lengthy song, usually called the *kommos*, in which Orestes, Electra and the chorus lament Agamemnon, appeal to him for support and summon him from the dead – a strange ritual combination of mourning and conjuration. Orestes is then told of Clytemnestra's dream which he interprets as a favourable omen for their enterprise, and, after the chorus sings an ode on the monstrousness of female transgression, Orestes finally knocks on the palace door, pretending to be a messenger with a report of Orestes' death. The preparation for the entrance to the palace, then, is not merely through the development of a plan of revenge and the explanation of motive. It is also prepared on the one hand through the reaffirmation of familial ties between brother and sister – and father, whose support from the grave is passionately invoked – and on the other hand through an extended series of ritual scenarios – the libation-pouring, the prayers and offerings, the *kommos* – which place the revenge within a context of ordered religious activity.

The murder of the queen, like that of the king in the *Agamemnon*, receives extended dramatization after its lengthy scenes of preparation. After Clytemnestra takes the unrecognized Orestes into the palace, surprisingly his old nurse comes out to summon Aegisthus; she laments Orestes' apparent death; she recalls his childhood. She is persuaded by the chorus to tell Aegisthus to come without his usual bodyguard – a striking example of a chorus' direct involvement in the action of the play. The chorus then sings a prayer to the gods for the success of revenge. Aegisthus returns, enters the house and is summarily dispatched by Orestes. The queen hears the cry of a servant and comes on stage pursued by Orestes: their confrontation thus takes place centre stage. She bares her breast and appeals for mercy, and, in a famous moment, Orestes hesitates and turns to his companion for advice with the classic tragic question 'What am I to do, Pylades?'. Pylades, hitherto silent – and silent for the rest of the play – speaks three magisterial lines reaffirming the need to follow the god's injunctions. Orestes drives his mother into the house; the chorus sings of the arrival of justice at last; and Orestes appears over the bodies of his mother and Aegisthus, just as Clytemnestra had appeared over the bodies of Agamemnon and Cassandra. While Orestes is speaking in justification of the killing (as had his mother), he sees the Furies approaching (though no one else can see them). As his wits fail him, he flees off-stage, leaving the chorus to wonder where it will all end.

In the *Choephoroi*, then, as in the *Agamemnon*, the central action of a man returning to his home, a double murder, committed by a trick, and the display of the corpses, is set in a complex series of contexts through commentary, ritual, prophecy and explanation.

This process continues in the *Eumenides*, where the murders are subject to further discussion leading up to their formal consideration in the trial scene. The *Eumenides* opens in Delphi, where a priestess is about to enter the shrine of Apollo and pray. The calm is broken as she exits from the shrine on all fours, terrified by the awful sight she has seen inside the shrine – the Furies. But before they are viewed by the audience, first Orestes is comforted by Apollo and sent, after ritual purification, to Athens, and Clytemnestra's ghost appears to exhort the Furies to pursue Orestes. The Furies awaken and enter, only to be sent from the shrine by Apollo. Rapid action; brief scenes for new and different characters; but the two sides of the conflict are firmly established: Orestes and Apollo; Clytemnestra and the Furies.

The scene moves to Athens, where Orestes prays to Athene for salvation; the chorus enters in pursuit. Orestes attempts to justify himself, but the Furies dismiss his pleas and begin to sing the 'binding song' – a spell that promises the violent and disgusting death of their victim as punishment for his transgressions. Athene, however, enters, agrees to preside over the case, hears the preliminary statements from both sides, and sets up a court of citizens to try the case. After a choral ode on the subject of justice (which I mentioned in the previous chapter) the trial takes place with the chorus cross-examining Orestes, and Apollo speaking in his defence, and then the jurors voting. Athene declares that if the votes are equal, Orestes will go free, and she adds her vote to Orestes' cause. The votes are indeed equal. He leaves, thanking the goddess and promising the help of Argos eternally for Athens. The Furies, however, turn in wrath against Athens. Athene, the goddess of Athens, persuades them to be mollified and to take up an honoured place in the *polis*. The Furies eventually accept, and the play ends with a procession and praise in honour of the new dispensation of the *polis*, its new sense of order and justice. The *Eumenides*, then, not only judges in a formal way the action central to the previous plays, but also offers resolution on a grand plane. Divinities are prosecutors and defence and judge; the city itself is the stake of the final conflicts and final triumph. The trilogy that starts with a lowly watchman of one house asking the gods for release from toil and waiting for a beacon light ends with a massive torch-lit procession in the centre of the *polis* itself, led by divinities.

The following three sections of this chapter offer different routes of exploring this narrative. First, I will look at three major structuring devices of the narrative; secondly, I will discuss some ways in which man's place in a social and political frame is articulated; finally I will consider some passages in detail to demonstrate how Aeschylean poetry functions.

A charter for the city?

6 Revenge: order and transgression

The *Oresteia* is dominated by a narrative pattern of revenge. 'Revenge' in modern Western culture may seem a somewhat restricted concern. In the hierarchical, competitive world of Greece, however, where 'do good deeds to your friend, and do bad deeds to your enemy' is a commonly espoused and enacted moral principle, revenge is in many ways a social norm. In the *Oresteia*, however, as in Shakespeare's *Hamlet*, the narrative of revenge is used to explore the nature of human action and obligation, as well as the broadest ideas of justice and transgression (from which revenge draws its force as a principle). As in *Hamlet*, the *Oresteia*'s focus on revenge within a single household leads to the tragedy of intrafamilial violence and conflicting obligations. The structure of the Aeschylean trilogy, however, also links this pattern of revenge to a pattern of *reversal*, where the very act of taking revenge repeatedly turns the revenger into an object of revenge, as the trilogy explores with extraordinary sophistication the ancient Greek proverb that 'He who acts is acted upon' (*Cho.* 313), or, as it is more commonly translated, 'the doer suffers'. Revenge, in the *Oresteia*, is always already part of a vendetta: 'Exacting its debt, vengeance shouts loud: let the payment for bloody blow be bloody blow' (*Cho.* 310–12). The concern with revenge, then, opens a vista of violence, obligation, punishment and justice – the very widest dynamics of social order.

Each of the play's central conflicts that I described briefly in the previous section needs to be carefully placed within this narrative of revenge and reversal. Let us begin with that central act of the *Agamemnon*, the murder of the king. First, Clytemnestra justifies her actions to the chorus in part at least as revenge for the death of her daughter, Iphigeneia. Iphigeneia, however, was sacrificed to enable the fleet of the Greek forces to sail to Troy to avenge the rape of Helen by Paris, the Trojan prince. Agamemnon and Menelaus, his brother and Helen's husband, are sent as a 'Fury against transgressors' (*Aga.* 59). The expedition is sent by Zeus Xenios, that is, Zeus, king of the gods, in his capacity as the protector of the proper relations between households ('Zeus of guest relations'). Paris' transgression against such ties is to be avenged. Yet the fleet is held up at Aulis by Artemis, a goddess. She is outraged at an omen that has been seen as the fleet is preparing to sail: two eagles eating a pregnant hare. Because of this, as the seer Calchas interprets, the goddess may demand 'another sacrifice' – the daughter of the king. Clytemnestra's killing, then, is claimed as revenge for the death of Iphigeneia, which is itself the product of a complex web of cause and consequence, transgression and punishment.

The story of Agamemnon's decision to sacrifice his daughter shows clearly how the action of taking revenge leads the revenger into a position of tragic conflict – and of transgression (Nussbaum). The chorus, who narrate the sacrifice of Iphigeneia as part of the history of the Trojan War's genesis, tell of the omen of the eagles and the hare, and of Calchas' interpretation of it. At that point, they turn suddenly to sing of Zeus, the king of the gods. It is, they sing, his law that 'knowledge comes from what happens to you' (*Aga.* 177); and 'from the gods grace is violent'. This harsh rule of divine power is immediately exemplified by Agamemnon, who is now depicted faced by a grim choice because of Artemis' demands: either he has to give up the expedition to avenge the adultery, or he has to sacrifice his daughter. This is the *locus classicus* of tragic choice (*Aga.* 206–11):

> A heavy fate not to obey
> But heavy if I am to rend my
>   child, glory of the household,
> Staining a father's hand
> With streams of virgin sacrifice near the altar.
>   What of this is without disaster?

Agamemnon knows that either course of action – and one must be chosen – is disastrous. This conflict of competing and necessary obligations is known as a tragic 'double bind'. The horror of the sacrifice is clear: the 'virgin sacrifice', by a 'father's hand', near 'the altar', stress both the religious transgression of human sacrifice and the familial horror of a father killing his daughter, 'glory of the *oikos*'. Yet he chooses the claims of the military expedition over the competing obligation: 'How could I become a deserter, failing the alliance?' (*Aga.* 212–13). So, if Agamemnon is to take revenge for Paris' transgression, he necessarily must transgress. This is the logic of the narrative of revenge and reversal.

And revenge he will have. As the messenger says (*Aga.* 532–3): 'Neither Paris, nor the city, bound to him in common cause, can boast their action is greater than what they have suffered.' The principle of 'the doer suffers' has been fully enacted for Paris and for Troy. And yet the messenger also reports the scattering of the Greek fleet, which, it is made clear, is the result of their desecration of the altars of the city of Troy. Paris' crime has led to his destruction. The Greek fleet's crime has led to its destruction. Agamemnon's killing of his daughter awaits requital. As Agamemnon returns to Clytemnestra's trap, then, he has been depicted both as a victor punishing transgression and as a transgressor awaiting punishment. From the first ode's representation of the sacrifice of Iphigeneia, Agamemnon is locked into a narrative of revenge and reversal: revenge which punishes wrongdoing, but which, in turn, establishes the revenger as a wrongdoer in need of punishment.

Cassandra, however, offers a further perspective on Agamemnon and his death. For in her prophecies she recalls the violent past of the house of Agamemnon. Agamemnon's father, Atreus, took revenge on his brother, Thyestes (who had commited adultery with Atreus' wife) by killing, cooking and serving to Thyestes his own children. There is, in Cassandra's vision (*Aga.* 1187–92), 'a band of celebrating furies who have drunk on human blood and sit in the house singing a song of the first and originating outrage'. There is in the house a violent past that also has an effect on the present action. The central act of the *Agamemnon*, Agamemnon's death, instantiates not only a pattern of transgression and revenge, but also a specific, inherited repetition of intrafamilial violence. So Aegisthus, in the final scene of the *Agamemnon*, boasts that his part in the king's death is a revenge for what Agamemnon's father, Atreus, had done to Thyestes, Aegisthus' father. Agamemnon is part of a family history he cannot escape.

Agamemnon's death, then, is overdetermined, that is, it is seen to be the result of several different patterns of revenge and reversal, familial horrors.

In her turn, Clytemnestra, the agent of Agamemnon's destruction, even as she boasts over the bodies of her victims, vainly hopes that 'the thrice gorged demon of the family' can be appeased. Her hopes are vain because Orestes, in the central conflict of the *Choephoroi*, returns to repeat the tragic double bind. Orestes suggests that a powerful set of motives drives him on (*Cho.* 299–305). He is fulfilling the god's command to exact vengeance, but he is also being forced to kill within his own family. As he drives Clytemnestra to her death, he sums up his position in his final, climactic line with (*Cho.* 930): 'You killed whom you ought not, now suffer what you ought not.' The logic of the double bind, of revenge and reversal, is starkly exposed. To punish wrong leads to doing wrong: not to punish wrong is also doing wrong. The doer suffers . . .

Indeed, when he, like his mother before him, appears above the corpses of his victims, Orestes in his turn moves from victor and punisher to victim and transgressor. The very instantiations of revenge and punishment, the Furies, appear and hound him off stage. The hunter is now hunted.

In the *Eumenides*, the Furies in their bloodthirsty pursuit of Orestes from Delphi to Athens seem set to continue this pattern of revenge and reversal to the point of the destruction of the male line of the house of Agamemnon. Yet the trial allows Orestes to escape punishment. And as the Furies turn in anger against Athens, Athene's persuasion assimilates them into the city, as guardians of order. On both the human and the divine level there is in the final scenes of the trilogy a move away from bloody conflict where each victory leads to disastrous transgression towards an institution and practice that aim to resolve conflict without transgressive destructiveness. As the narrative has been motivated by a pattern of transgression and punishment, so the narrative ends with the discovery of the potential to avoid the unending violence of revenge and reversal.

'The doer suffers', then, is a repeated pattern of tragic action that structures the narrative of the *Oresteia*. In punishing a wrong, Agamemnon, Clytemnestra, Orestes, each commits a wrong, and thus becomes the hunter hunted, the sacrificer sacrificed, the punisher punished. Each, too, recognizes the tragic dilemma that leads to such inevitable transgression. The paradox of the double bind is central to the plotting of the *Oresteia*.

The language with which the figures in the trilogy comment on this action, however, binds this narrative of tragic action with the very widest ideas of justice and social order. Again, I will need a Greek word for my argument, and that word is *dikē*. This is one of the most important and pervasive words of fifth-century Greek. Its range of sense runs from abstract ideas of 'justice' or 'right', through 'retribution', 'punishment' to the particular legal senses of 'law-court' and 'law-case'. It is a fundamental term for the expression of social order in that it both indicates the proper organization of society as a whole, and delineates right action for individuals and the institution through which such order is to be maintained. Thus, for example, Plato's *Republic*, a description of a society organized on philosophical principles, is expressly formulated as the search for a *polis* founded according to *dikē* – yet it is also *dikē*, say, to treat one's parents with respect; and it is through *dikē* – the process of law – that social order is enacted and social conflicts contested.

The word *dikē*, and words derived from it, are used obsessively in the *Oresteia* to gloss the narrative of revenge. So, for example, Paris is described as 'the man who kicked the altar of *dikē*' (*Aga.* 382–3); *dikē* is said to enforce Zeus's rule that 'learning comes from experience' (*Aga.* 250–1); the destruction of Troy is from 'Zeus who brings *dikē*' (*Aga.* 525–6); Agamemnon sees himself as the agent of *dikē* in the destruction of Troy (*Aga.* 813); Clytemnestra sees herself as the agent of *dikē* in the destruction of Agamemnon (*Aga.* 1432); the chorus warns that '*Dikē* is being sharpened to new deeds of harm on new whetstones of fate' (*Aga.* 1535–6). So, in the *Choephoroi*, Orestes arrives as an agent of *dikē* (*Cho.* 641–5); and the chorus sings that (*Cho.* 931) '*Dikē* came to the sons of Priam in time . . .' and so to the house of Agamemnon has come *dikē*, the daughter of Zeus. Electra, however, expressly introduces a distinction: when she is exhorted by the chorus to pray for the arrival of a saviour, she asks if they mean (*Cho*. 120) 'a juror or someone who brings retribution', a **dik***astes* or a **dikē***phoros*. The chorus retorts that they just want someone to kill in return, but Electra's distinction looks forward to the *Eumenides*, where the Furies' pursuit of *dikē*, retribution, leads to a trial, *dikai*, before jurors, *dikastai*, who evaluate the justice, *dikē*, of the case. 'Revere the altar of *dikē*', sings the chorus (*Eum*. 539), recalling the language used of Paris' transgression in the *Agamemnon*. And it is finally with the *dikē* of the city that the *Oresteia* ends (*Eum*. 993–4).

From even these few examples, it can be seen how the narrative of revenge and reversal, as it moves towards the law-court, is articulated in the language of *dikē*. This has led to what is still a standard reading of the trilogy, namely, that the *Oresteia* traces a transformation from *dikē* as revenge to *dikē* as legal justice – a move from the bloody repetition of vendetta to the ordered world of the *polis* and its institutions. Thus the *Oresteia* on this view offers a sort of myth of origin of the institution of law so important, as we have seen, to the development of the city and its democracy. A charter for the city . . .

Let me sketch in slightly more detail this interpretation, following H. D. F. Kitto's eloquent version. In the *Agamemnon*, 'there is a law of Dikē – not "justice" but "requital" – that wrongs done must have their revenge, "the doer must pay"'. 'Agamemnon has taken it for granted that a war for a wanton woman is a proper thing: it is his conception of Dikē. It is also Zeus' conception and Zeus is going to follow it by destroying the destroyer.' Thus the tragic double bind of Agamemnon is seen as a flaw in the idea of *dikē*: 'The obvious implication is that we have a conception of Dikē that cannot work even though it is the present will of Zeus. The instinct for violent and bloody retribution dominates and unifies the whole play and in the end it leads to a complete breakdown.'

The implications of this 'unworkable' notion of *dikē* are developed in the *Choephoroi*, as Orestes approaches the task of avenging his father. For even if Electra prays to be 'purer by far than my mother' (*Cho*. 140–1) and worries about the distinction between 'a juror' and 'one who brings retribution', even if Orestes aims to return his house to the norms of patriarchal rule, the sense of direct retribution remains dominant: 'Only the kinsmen can set the family free. "Ares (violence) will confront Ares; Dikē will confront Dikē" (*Cho.* 461). But if Dikē conflicts with Dikē . . . the universe is chaotic, and Dikē cannot yet be "Justice".' There is, for Kitto, still chaos at the heart of the notion of *dikē* as it is instantiated in the *Choephoroi*'s violent retribution.

The trial scene of the *Eumenides* replaces such retribution with the possibility of mediation. Athene transcends the opposition of Apollo and the Furies, and brings to the trial 'tolerance, level judgement'. What the reconciliation of the final scenes indicates is that 'wrath . . . as the means of Dikē, gives place to Reason' – and at the level of the divine 'Zeus has moved forward from violence and confusion . . . to reason and mercy.' The cosmic order mirrors the order of the *polis*: 'the problem of Dikē is solved'.

This approach to the *Oresteia* has been dominant for many years. It offers a vision of the *Oresteia* moving from tragic problems to a resolution in the harmony of achieved social order, from violence to mediation, from the darkness and despair of the corrupt house to the shining glories of the city of Athens (Meier). It sees the *Oresteia* making the transition from the false light of the beacons to the true light of the final torch-lit procession of the Athenians. This reading of the trilogy has been opposed mainly by Marxist and feminist critics, who have seen the 'justice' at the end of the work not as a triumph of reasoned civilization but as an evolution towards the apparatus of state authority on the one hand, and towards the enforcement of patriarchal authority on the other (Goldhill 1984, 1986). For these readings too the *Oresteia* depicts a transition towards the order of legal justice – but the order of legal justice is itself seen as a difficult ideological projection rather than as a simply laudable 'social order'. Yet there are problems with seeing the *Oresteia* in this way as simply evolutionary (whether towards 'social justice' or 'power for the few masked as social justice'), and there are three particular areas of difficulty I wish to look at.

The first is the trial itself. I have mentioned the importance of law to democracy; and there is no doubt that the trial is crucial to allowing Orestes' freedom. Yet it must not be forgotten that the trial's vote is equal. As an institution, it mirrors the doubts and difficulties of the previous conflicts of the trilogy. What is more, the Furies are so outraged at the decision that they threaten the city of Athens itself with destruction. It is the persuasion of Athene rather than the trial that leads to the end of this narrative and its celebrations. Indeed, over a third of the *Eumenides* remains after Orestes leaves. So the ending of this play is not with the institution of legal justice as force for resolution, but with a goddess' persuasion and the lauding of the *polis*. It is not the legal process itself which resolves the tensions of the *Oresteia*.

The second problem is that each of the major conflicts of the play is perceived as a clash of competing obligations: for Agamemnon it is the competing claims of his military role as leader of the Trojan expedition and his familial role as father and husband; for Orestes, his desire to take up his rightful position in a properly ordered house is in opposition to a requirement to transgress the basic ties of a properly ordered house; for Clytemnestra, her desire to avenge her daughter leads her to transgress her duty to her husband. The *Oresteia*, that is, uncovers ways in which obligations within a social frame can come into conflict with one another, and can lead to tragedy. This uncomfortable vision remains throughout the trilogy, and is not resolved by the play's ending. The *Oresteia* shows the potential for violent conflict of interest within the obligations of social order.

The third problem is perhaps most important, and it relates closely to the sense of 'the tragic moment' I discussed earlier. It concerns the language of *dikē* which, it is claimed, articulates the move from vendetta to law. The difficulty can be succinctly expressed: the language of *dikē* is far more intricate and far more opaque than this evolutionary approach suggests. I will just offer two of the many possible examples. The first is from the entrance of Agamemnon in the *Agamemnon*. I described above the preparation for his arrival as conqueror who has punished and as transgressor being led towards retribution. Here are his first words (*Aga.* 810–16):

> To Argos first and to the gods of the land
> It is right (*dikē*) I give due greeting; they have worked with me
> To bring me home. They helped me on the vengeance (*dikē*)
> I have wrought
> On Priam's city. Not from the tongues of men the gods
> Heard justice (*dik-*) but in one unhesitating cast they laid
> Their votes within the urn of blood.

The triple repetition of *dikē* and *dikaios* (the adjective from *dikē*) in three consecutive lines is strongly marked. In the first instance, *dikē* seems to imply a general standard of correct behaviour for the king with regard to the gods ('It is *right* . . .'). In the second case, it seems to imply the retribution of blood for blood ('vengeance . . .'). But in the third case, *dikē* (in the plural) implies 'cases', 'pleas' ('heard justice . . .'), as, indeed, the voting of the gods in urns suggests a legal procedure that looks forward to the *Eumenides*. Even the phrase for 'unhesitatingly' punningly echoes the repetitions of *dik-* in the previous lines: *ou **dik**horropos*. Aristotle derives the word *dikē* precisely from this term's root (*dikha* = 'separately', 'in two parts'). So as the king enters, there is a complex interplay of different senses of the word *dikē* that cannot be subsumed under the simple notion of revenge or retribution. The evolutionary view of the trilogy has to ignore such complexities of language to maintain its sense of clear development.

My second example is a line I quoted above from Kitto's analysis, one that is often used by critics, and it shows clearly how such complexities of language are ignored in practice. 'Ares (violence) will confront Ares; *dikē* will confront *dikē*' (*Cho.* 461). Kitto comments: 'If Dikē conflicts with Dikē . . . the universe is chaotic, and Dikē cannot yet be "Justice".' Yet the very next line reads 'O Gods, be just (*dik-*) in what you bring about.' The gods are exhorted to bring things to pass in a just way (*en**dik**ōs*), that is, an appeal is made to precisely the ordered, general standard of right that the previous line was quoted to show as absolutely lacking! The chaos of conflict is not the neat clash of right and right, so much as the juxtaposition of a line proclaiming such a clash to a line maintaining a criterion of judgement for that clash constructed in the selfsame vocabulary. A sense of violent incoherence is produced not because a sense of 'Justice' is lacking, but because an *excess* of meaning is produced by these juxtaposed uses of *dikē*.

The language of *dikē*, then, cannot be so neatly controlled as 'the move from vendetta to law' would suggest. Aeschylus displays the complex and contrasting senses of the term throughout the trilogy. This is what I meant earlier when I talked of tragedy dramatizing different and competing ideals, different and competing senses of words. Aeschylus shows not how 'the problem of *Dikē* is solved', but rather how problems remain inherently active in the ambiguities and difficulties of the term itself.

This leads to an important, more general argument. What the two passages above show is how different characters at different times in the trilogy appeal to *dikē* as a criterion, support or reason for action. Indeed, every character declares *dikē* to be on his or her side, makes a one-sided claim to this key evaluative term. In this way, tragedy explores how normal, political, evaluative language is used within social conflict, and becomes a source of social conflict. Yet as tragedy dramatizes the blockages and barriers of humans trying to communicate with this evaluative language, an audience of the play is put in an extraordinary position. From one perspective, an audience can see how words take on different meanings, depending on who uses them and how. From another perspective, an audience can appreciate the widest range of meaning, even as it can see a particular character using a term in a particular way. This not only produces a particular depth and semantic resonance in tragic language, but also works to uncover the tensions and ambiguities within the evaluative vocabulary of society. This is nowhere more strongly felt than in the *Oresteia* where the language of *dikē* – social order, right – is fragmented and split under Aeschylus' tragic scrutiny.

We are now in a position to appreciate the *Oresteia*'s particular complexity. On the one hand, it dramatizes human agents engaged in a tragic narrative of revenge and reversal, where each event is intricately connected with every other, and each action involves a double bind of conflicting obligations. On the other hand, the language of social order, in which the narrative is to be understood, is itself shown to be full of unresolved tensions and ambiguities. The story of revenge, then, is used to explore the formation and transgression of social order. It is in this way, first of all, that the *Oresteia* speaks to the *polis*.

7 *The female is slayer of the male . . .*

This exploration of social order and transgression, however, is also markedly constructed in terms of gender. At every point in the narrative, events are expressed as conflicts between men and women, male and female. So Cassandra sums up the narrative of revenge and reversal (*Aga*. 1318–19): 'But after my death, bear me witness, when a woman dies for me a woman, and when there falls an ill-wed man for a man', and the murder of Agamemnon is seen as (*Aga*. 1231–2): 'The female is slayer of the male . . .'

The focus on gender starts in the opening speech where Clytemnestra's posting of the watchman is described with 'Such is the authority of the man-plotting heart of the woman.' The word 'authority' (*kratos*) in Greek is associated in particular with male power, firstly within the household. The *oikos* (unlike the democratic *polis*) is a hierarchical system with the father – the man – in charge. The subordination of the wife to the husband, female to male, that we have seen as a determining factor in the definition of citizenship in Athens, is also a fundamental element of the order of the *oikos*. Indeed, throughout a woman's life, she is legally and socially under the authority of a particular male, first her father or other male guardian and second her husband, eventually, even, her son. So, to describe a woman as a figure of authority immediately points to a strange connection of gender and power in this narrative. So, too, the juxtaposition of the terms 'woman' and 'man-plotting' emphasizes that it is the expectations of gender that make a woman's authority out of place. Indeed, the adjective I have translated 'man-plotting' can mean both 'plotting like a man' and 'plotting against a man'. The double sense is significant: for a woman to plot *like* a man – and thus aim at the position of authority – is inevitably to plot *against* a man: against the established order of patriarchy.

The focus on Clytemnestra, her gender and her power, continues unabated throughout the *Agamemnon*. In the first scene, as she enters, the chorus says (*Aga*. 255): 'I come in honour of your authority (*kratos*), Clytemnestra' – and immediately explains: 'for it is right to honour the wife of a ruler, if the throne lacks a male'. The lack of a 'male' – the widest gender term – is the reason why a woman's authority can be considered. So, after the queen has finally persuaded the chorus of the beacon's import, they say (*Aga*. 351): 'Woman, you are speaking like a sensible man . . .' This is picked up when the messenger enters to confirm Clytemnestra's proclamation, and she taunts the chorus for failing to believe her 'as a woman' (*Aga*. 592). It is not surprising, then, when Agamemnon, as he is being persuaded to walk across the tapestries to his house, says to Clytemnestra (*Aga.* 940): 'It is not a woman's part to desire battle.' He sees her desire as a wish to play a male role, battle, warfare; and if he is being ironic in his use of such language for what is as yet a war of words, he will shortly discover the aptness of such terminology when she kills him in his bath with a male military weapon.

Clytemnestra indeed dominates the *Agamemnon*. How does her representation relate to the expectations of a woman's role? There are two particular ways that the figure of Clytemnestra is constructed as transgressive, her use of language and her sexual behaviour. Let us look at both in turn.

Now in democratic Athens, as we have seen, there was little public role for women. Despite the function of women in certain religious ceremonies, neither Assembly nor law-court allowed women any speaking role. Indeed, the association of women with the inside of the house, private and unseen, is pervasive in Greek writing. For a woman to appear in public as a speaker, except within a closely controlled religious context, is in itself a sign of a woman out of place (Foley; Gould 1980). Clytemnestra takes this to an extreme. Not only does she dominate the stage as the play's main and most impressive speaker, but also deception, persuasion, guile – the manipulation of language – is the route to her domination. There is commonly an association of the female with corrupt language in early Greek thought (Arthur), or with especially privileged language, such as prophecy, religious utterance. Clytemnestra takes to an extreme the fear and power associated with such misuse of words.

Yet it is also as a sexually corrupt woman that Clytemnestra is figured. There is throughout the Greek world little interest in the sort of psychological tales of adultery familiar through modern Western literature: personal fulfilment through emotional satisfaction plays a far more restricted role in fifth-century Athens than in post-Romantic culture (Tanner). Adultery is perceived more as a social threat. Thus, Helen's adultery requires a full military expedition from Greece to take revenge, and it has implications throughout the fabric of society. Helen's 'daring the undareable' is not only the background to Agamemnon's absence; it is also a model to illumine her sister Clytemnestra's behaviour. The common ideological association of the woman with the inside of the house (which I mentioned

in the previous paragraph) is represented repeatedly in Greek writing as a necessary response to the threat of women's desires leading
to adultery; and this adultery is represented as a threat to the se-
cure pattern of male inheritance within a patriarchal social system.
The threat of the misuse of the female body is a threat to the social
position of the male. The maintenance of the *oikos*, then – its generational continuity, the status of its property – depends on the proper
restraint of its women. ('Proper', 'property', 'propriety' is no chance
collocation of vocabulary . . .) So, 'marriage is the cornerstone of
society'. Or, 'patriarchy requires the sexual control of women'.

This is summed up nowhere more clearly than in the central ode
of the central play of the trilogy, where the chorus, singing of the
monstrous desires of women, pronounce (*Cho.* 599–601):

> Desire, corrupt desire, female in power,
> Perverts and conquers the yoked society
> Of beasts and men.

The desire of women is corrupt; it is *thēlukratēs*. I have translated
this word 'female in power'; it implies that such desire gives women
power (*kratos*); or that desire overpowers women; or that desire for
the female overpowers marriages; or desire empowers women to
pervert and conquer. This negative desire destroys the 'yoked society
of beasts and men' – that is, all forms of union that make up society.
It is this threat that Clytemnestra embodies.

Clytemnestra's pursuit of power, then, through her misuse of
words and her misuse of her body in adultery constructs a figure of
monstrous reversal of the female role. One effect of this representation of the woman in charge is the great reduction of the role of
Aegisthus. In the *Agamemnon*, he appears only in the last scene – a
bathetic, if aggressive figure – where he is despised by the erstwhile
ineffective chorus and called 'woman'. This symmetry of radical
opposition – as the woman becomes man-like the man becomes
feminized – is typical both of Aeschylus' stark structural composition, and of the Greek tendency towards polarization where the
'only alternative to rule by men is rule by women' (Zeitlin). The conflict between Agamemnon and Clytemnestra thus remains sharply
focused as a struggle between a man and a woman, husband and
wife, king and queen, male and female.

A similar focusing can be seen in the *Choephoroi*. The language of gender remains to the fore (as the chorus discussed above shows), and Aegisthus receives even less stage time than in the *Agamemnon*. He enters, speaks only fourteen lines – ironically about how no one can pull the wool over his eyes – and goes to meet his doom unsuspectingly in the palace. After his death, he is scarcely mentioned. The killing of Aegisthus is not an issue.

Electra is a more complicated figure, however. The daughter of marriageable age in the house is an object of particular concern: she is at the moment of transition between statuses (daughter/wife; adolescent (*parthenos*)/woman), at the point of transition between houses (from father's to husband's). The daughter of a corrupt house is in an anomalous position, however, forced to wait in such a transitional state for the return of order to the *oikos*. Electra prays to be 'purer by far than my mother', and it is clear that she struggles to play the role of the good daughter. It is here that the ritual focus of the first part of the *Choephoroi* takes on an added importance. I have mentioned that there is no public position from which a woman can speak without being out of place – except religion. The extensive performance of religious rites in this play is co-extensive with Electra's speaking role. As the revenge approaches, she is sent inside by Orestes. And so to silence. She is thus returned to the proper place of the unmarried daughter – on the inside – to await the outcome of the man's attempt to reorder the *oikos*. In terms of the normative expectations of gender roles, then, Electra is set in opposition to Clytemnestra.

Aegisthus and Electra are thus removed from the scene to allow a more intense concentration on the opposition of Orestes and Clytemnestra, son and mother, male and female, centre stage. And indeed their face-to-face encounter also revolves around gender roles. Clytemnestra appeals against the double standard that allows Agamemnon's adultery and killings but stigmatizes hers. Orestes replies with a repeated reinforcement of precisely such a polarized division of gender roles (*Cho.* 919, 921): 'The woman who sits on the inside must not reprove the man who labours', 'The toil of a man nourishes the women who sit inside.' To kill his mother is for Orestes also to re-establish the proper boundaries of behaviour for men and women.

The *Eumenides* continues this opposition. Apollo, a male god, supports Orestes; the Furies, female figures, support Clytemnestra's cause. The trial itself turns on issues central to gender roles. For Apollo's final and necessary argument (*Cho.* 657–61) is that the mother is no parent to the child; the true parent is 'the one who mounts', and the mother is just 'like a host for the male seed'. So too Athene's reasons for voting for Orestes are explicitly based on her support for 'the male in all things' (*Eum.* 737). I shall return to this debate shortly.

First, however, I wish to emphasize the effect such a focus has on the narrative of revenge and reversal. At each point of the narrative where tragic conflict takes place, this conflict is depicted as a conflict between the genders. Agamemnon, sent by Zeus, a god, hindered by Artemis, a goddess, is forced to choose between becoming the slayer of his daughter or deserting the men of the military expedition to avenge his brother. Clytemnestra is faced by Agamemnon, to be a husband killer to avenge her daughter. Orestes is faced by Clytemnestra, to be a mother killer to avenge his father. Apollo, a god, faces the Furies, female divinities, in a trial which turns on who is the true parent, the male or the female.

What is more, at each point in these conflicts the female tends towards the support of a position and arguments that are based on the values of ties of blood to the point of the rejection of the ties of society, whereas the male tends to support a wider outlook of social relations to the exclusion of the claims of family and blood. Thus Agamemnon sacrifices his own daughter, 'glory of the household', to enable the panhellenic fleet to sail. He rejects his duties as a father to maintain his position in society as king and leader of an international military force. Clytemnestra rejects the social tie of marriage, both by killing her husband and by her adultery, in part at least to avenge her daughter. Orestes rejects that apparently most 'natural' of blood ties, between mother and son, to regain his patrimony and reassert the social order of patriarchy. Apollo is a god of state religion, the great civilizer from the international oracle at Delphi. The Furies are depicted as female who seem ready to ignore any claim of society in their pursuit of those who have killed their own kin, their own blood.

The seemingly endless pattern of revenge and reversal, then, is also a pattern of male–female opposition, that itself tends towards an opposition of social and political obligations to familial and blood ties.

Let us now return to the final scenes of the trilogy. Apollo's argument, in support of Orestes' action, seeks to remove the female from any significant role in the production of children (and we may here remember the story of 'birth from the soil' which I mentioned in the opening chapter as part of the Athenians' charter myths). The Furies seek to ignore any mitigating circumstances or reasoning for an act of intrafamilial violence. It is clear that the opposition of Apollo and the Furies stresses in an extreme form the radical opposition of male and female, social ties and blood ties. What then, of Athene? She is, of course, a goddess; but she is a goddess who has many of the attributes associated with masculinity in the fifth century. She is a warrior who wears armour and fights; she is associated with the head, as a goddess of wisdom and of guile, and because she sprang fully armed from the head of her father Zeus. She is also a virgin goddess without a male partner. This strange status of Athene must be remembered when she gives her reasons for voting for Orestes – reasons which are instrumental in his preservation and thus the trilogy's conclusion (*Eum.* 735–41):

> I will cast this vote for Orestes.
> For no mother exists who bore me.
> I favour the male in all things, except in attaining marriage,
> With all my spirit. I am wholly of the father.
> Thus I will not privilege the fate of a woman
> Who has killed her husband, the overseer of the house.

Athene's reasons start from the fact that she has no mother. The importance of parental relations has, of course, been emphasized throughout the trilogy, and here Athene is separated from any associations with a mother, with a female line, with female blood. She favours 'the male' – note the general category – in all things with all her spirit, except for marriage, that is, except for the one basic role assigned to females within a rigidly patriarchal order. Athene who favours the male does not conform to the female's role within the male dispensation. Thus, she concludes, she is 'wholly of the father'. I have used this rather strange phrase in English to try to capture some of the range of the Greek, which implies 'I am wholly my father's child' (as Athene can claim to be); 'I am wholly on the side of the father', that is, in any conflict between a mother's and a father's rights; 'I am a faithful follower of my father' (Apollo has claimed that Zeus ordered and supports Orestes' actions). The combination is significant, linking as it does the specifics of Athene's status and Orestes' case to the general social position of 'the father' in patriarchy. This collection of reasons leads directly ('thus') to her conclusion, that she cannot grant respect to a woman who has killed her husband, who is 'overseer of the house', that is, who holds the authority and status of master within the *oikos*.

Athene's vote, then, has two crucial aspects. On the one hand, it is given for reasons fundamentally linked to the social expectations of gender. Athene supports Orestes because of the unchallengeable role of the man as head of the household, with all the implications of such authority for the position of 'the father' and for the status of 'the male'. On the other hand, the vote is delivered by someone who fits uneasily into such categorizations: a virgin warrior goddess, a female without links to the mother, a female who does not enter marriage. As the narrative has been structured around the polarized oppositions of the genders, so the narrative's ending depends on a figure who does not fit easily into such an opposition.

This may help us to see how her conflict with the Furies ends in resolution. For the first time in the trilogy we do not have the polarized opposition of male and female, each seeking for dominance. Rather, it is an opposition of this strange figure, Athene, and the female Furies, where Athene is aiming at reconciliation rather than at victory through destruction. The diffusion of the rigid and sharply focused opposition of male and female helps achieve the trilogy's conclusion, as it has motivated its action throughout.

Athene persuades the Furies to be assimilated into her city Athens, but the status they are to hold is expressly that of 'metics', resident aliens. They are to remain apart from the city in which they are to play a part. Since the Furies have come to stand not merely for the claims of punishment for transgression but also for the claims of blood ties and the female, this positioning has often been seen as particularly significant. For Kitto and those who follow his line of interpretation, this resolution represents the transcendence of Apollo's rejection of the role of the female, and a recognition for the city of the necessary place for what the Furies represent. For an

extensive tradition of feminist scholarship, this conclusion represents rather the justification of a subordinate position for the claims
of the Furies – with an obvious social analogue for the position of
women in Athens. The *Oresteia* becomes viewed as a complex example of what anthropologists have called the 'myth of matriarchy
overturned', that is, a story that tells of the overthrow of female authority or female search for power as a way of justifying the continuing status quo of male authority in society (Bamberger). Certainly,
the final scenes of the trilogy praise the *polis* and its logic of control
of women, established laws of marriage, production of legitimate
children and restricted rights of women within the state. Yet before
the play is taken just as a reaffirmation of the city's order, it must
be remembered first that this resolution is effected by Athene, a figure whose representation – even as the goddess of Athens – offers
such a complex example for the norms of gender roles; and secondly,
that this representation of Athene – as male-like, warrior, persuasive female – comes perilously close to the figure of Clytemnestra
(Winnington-Ingram). Whatever the sense of triumph and reconciliation at the end of the *Oresteia*, there remains a powerful sense of
potential transgression within the system of gender relations.

As the narrative of revenge and reversal moves towards the
polis, its law-court and the blessings of civic order, so the narrative
of gender develops its conflicts towards a resolution on the widest
political stage; gender and politics (inevitably) interpenetrate. Both
the thematic concern with violence and the thematic concern with
gender lead to the final scene's praise of the *polis* as the condition
of possibility of a good life. To appreciate the thrust of Aeschylus'
combination of violence, politics and gender, however, a further aspect needs to be considered, namely, the relation of this story to the
great epic of Homer, the *Odyssey*, and that is where I shall turn for
the next section of this chapter.

8 Homer and Aeschylus: rewriting the past for the present

Homer held a privileged place in Greek and Athenian culture.
The great epics, the *Iliad* and the *Odyssey*, were written down in a
canonical form in the time of Peisistratus. In the fifth century, they

played an integral role in the education, institutions and ideology of Athens, and indeed in the culture of all Greece as panhellenic epics (Nagy). Homer was the text first learnt and most studied at all levels of Greek education, and any educated Athenian could be expected to have a knowledge of it. Sections of the epic were regularly to be heard in performance, recited at symposia, say, or other festive occasions (a character in Xenophon's dialogue, the *Symposium*, talks of hearing such a recital every day), and on the occasion of the Great Panathenaia, a major festival in Athens in honour of the day of Athene's birth, the whole epics were delivered by professional performers called rhapsodes in the theatre. Each rhapsode was required to pick up the narrative from where the previous one had finished, and, typically, the performances were judged as a competition. The same character in Xenophon – although not a rhapsode – claims to know Homer off by heart, and praises such learning as an education in itself.

Homer was also a prime source of authority for knowledge, behaviour, ethics. He is regularly quoted in support of arguments, characters from Homer offer models of behaviour, and almost any situation could be related back to the privileged model of Homer. In this way, the Homeric texts were essential not only to the actual process of teaching and to the festival institutions of Athens, but also to the make-up of Athenian social attitudes and understanding: 'He was "the poet" . . . who had produced images of human experience that were true and right and timeless, in a variety of modes, and with a mastery and sophistication that were for Aeschylus, Sophocles and Euripides their education' (Gould 1983). Even though Athenian religion did not have 'sacred texts', it is with some justification that Homer has been called the Greek Bible – especially if one thinks, for example, of the use of the Bible in Victorian Britain: read after dinner, used in schools, a subject of heated academic debate, a cultural background widely diffused through different échelons of society, a much quoted source of moral and social guidance etc.

The cultural force of Homer continued to be dominant in democratic Athens, despite the evident differences between the heroic society portrayed in the *Iliad* and the *Odyssey* and the social system of the fifth-century *polis*. This is particularly striking if one compares, say, the individualistic heroes of Homer, each fighting for personal glory, and the democratic warrior praised by Pericles with his shared commitment to the *polis*. Many tragedies deal with aspects of these differences. But for my present purposes it is specifically the way that the *Oresteia* relates to the *Odyssey* that is important. For the story of Orestes is told no fewer than nine times in the first twelve books of the *Odyssey*, and referred to periodically afterwards as well. Although other versions of Orestes' story no doubt existed, it is against Homer's privileged model that Aeschylus is best understood.

Let me begin with how the story of Orestes comes to be told so often in the *Odyssey*. The plot of the *Odyssey*, at one level at any rate, is easy to describe. Odysseus has been prevented for ten years from returning home to Ithaca after the fall of Troy. His son, Telemachus, is on the point of manhood. His wife, Penelope, is besieged by suitors, who have moved into Odysseus' home in the absence of a male figure of authority, and are encouraging Penelope to remarry. The story of the *Odyssey* tells of Odysseus' return, how he and Telemachus rid the house of the suitors, and how Odysseus is reunited with his family and returns to his position as master of the house.

This story is told in a highly intricate and sophisticated manner, with flashbacks, disguises, lies, stories within stories, and all the narrative devices that have led to the *Odyssey* being seen as the forerunner to the modern novel. One theme of the work which is of particular interest here is the *Odyssey*'s concern with proper behaviour – particularly sexual behaviour – within the household. This theme is seen on many levels in the epic. At one level, the suitors transgress a range of social norms, not least in wooing Penelope and sleeping with her servants. They – and the maidservants – suffer the vengeance of the return of the rightful master and meet a grisly and violent end. At another level, Odysseus on his travels meets different sorts of figures and visits different societies. Each different society offers a different insight into the world of Ithaca. On the one hand, the wild, the violent, the monstrous – like the Cyclops – construct a negative image of a transgressive world where social values are flouted, and violent deception corrupts any normal process of communication. On the other, the Phaeacians live in a glorious and glamorous world where the trees are always in fruit, ships are self-propelling and even the guard-dogs are magic creatures of gold made by a god. The Phaeacians inhabit a society as excessive in its attributes of civilization as the Cyclops is without them. Both sorts of society have to be left behind by Odysseus. Both sorts of society help define – positively and negatively – the world of Ithaca to which Odysseus is returning. On a further level, Telemachus too travels around the Greek world, visiting different human societies trying to find out about his father. His journey is also a journey that instructs him in the business of adult social interaction. At all these three levels, the *Odyssey* is saying something about man in society, defining his place, exploring the norms and transgressions. And the first word of the epic is indeed 'man' – its subject defined from the start. It is this normative – the way it projects norms – thrust of the *Odyssey* that encourages the paradigmatic, didactic role it plays in the fifth century.

Now, the story of Orestes is always told in the *Odyssey* to be exemplary. The story is told to Telemachus to tell him how properly to be a young man; it is told to Odysseus to warn him of the perils of women and returning home. Orestes starts his life in literature as an example. The similarities between the house of Odysseus and the house of Agamemnon are repeatedly drawn. As Aegisthus corrupted Clytemnestra and took control of Agamemnon's home, so the suitors threaten Penelope in order to take control of Odysseus' house. As Agamemnon came home to a corrupt house to be murdered in a trap, so Odysseus is returning to a corrupted house and thus must use every trick and stratagem to avoid the traps of the suitors. As Orestes was threatened with the loss of his position as son and heir, so Telemachus is threatened by the suitors with the loss of his patrimony. So, Telemachus is exhorted by Athene, Nestor and Menelaus to prove himself a noble young man, act like Orestes, and save his patrimony. So, Odysseus is warned not to fall into the error of Agamemnon.

There is, however, in this story in the *Odyssey* a focus wholly different from Aeschylus' *Oresteia*. First, the conflicts of the epic are between men for authority within the house. It is Aegisthus who seduces Clytemnestra, sets the guard to watch for Agamemnon, kills Agamemnon – with the help of Clytemnestra's guile – takes control of the house and is killed by Orestes. Aegisthus is the first example of human behaviour discussed in the *Odyssey*. Orestes kills the usurper just as Telemachus and Odysseus will kill the usurping suitors. Clytemnestra is called 'deceptive' and in this capacity aids the plan of Agamemnon's death: so in Book 24 – finally and only there – she is said by a bitter Agamemnon to have killed her husband. But otherwise she is represented as a passive figure in the narrative of seduction and destruction. Penelope, for all her guile, is sent upstairs to wait in her room, while the men downstairs struggle for control of the *oikos*. Throughout the *Odyssey*, indeed, it is only in the wild world of Odysseus' travels that we see female figures of power – it is indeed a sign of that wildness.

A corollary of this focus is the striking silence on the matter of Clytemnestra's death. Although the Orestes story is told so many times, there is only one mention of Clytemnestra's death, and then by implication merely (*Od.* 3.307–10): 'In the eighth year, god-like Orestes came back from Athens and killed the murderer, guileful Aegisthus, who had killed his famous father. And when he had killed him, he invited the Argives for a funeral feast for his hated mother and cowardly Aegisthus.' The way that the tale moves from a masculine singular subject and object of killing ('when *he* had killed *him* . . . who had killed his famous father') to a plural funeral feast leaves a marked gap in the narrative. On the one hand, this wording may remind us of a significant difference between Telemachus and Orestes. Orestes can simply kill Aegisthus and regain his position; Telemachus' parents are alive and even after the death of the suitors he has to learn to take up a position not as master in sole and glorious control of his *oikos*, but as son and heir to Odysseus. On the other hand, the absence of any mention of matricide maintains both the positive image of Orestes and a focus on the male struggle for the control of the household. Indeed, although Odysseus returns as king, and although his revenge has implications throughout Ithacan society (since he kills many of its most well-born young men), the focus of the *Odyssey* remains first and foremost on the proper and controlled order of the household. One of the final images of the work is particularly telling. Odysseus, Laertes his father, and Telemachus are pictured standing and fighting together against the relatives of the slaughtered suitors – three generations of men, one exemplary home, the male line preserved, the embodiment of patriarchal authority. For Homer's *Odyssey*, both the transgressions that motivate the narrative of return and revenge, and the resolutions of these transgressions, are to be located in the order of the *oikos*.

When we move to Aeschylus, the focus on gender that I discussed in the previous section is now clearly to be seen as a *change* of focus. It is not Aegisthus but Clytemnestra who sets the watchman; it is Clytemnestra who tricks Agamemnon, kills Agamemnon, takes control of the house, and is the prime object of revenge. As we noted before, the death of Aegisthus – in the *Oresteia* as opposed to in Homer – is simply not an issue. There are, of course, many changes of plotting and detail between Homer and Aeschylus. But this overall shift of focus leads to two crucial points.

The first is this. If Clytemnestra's death was passed over in silence by Homer, it becomes the central, staged confrontation of the central play of Aeschylus' trilogy. Where, for Homer, Orestes is an example to be held up to the young Telemachus of how to be a noble man, for Aeschylus Orestes is the paradigmatic example of the tragic double bind. After Aeschylus, no one ever again says 'Be like Orestes!' (the famous matricide). Aeschylus has taken the key example of a key text and made that example problematic. He uncovers from the silence of Homer a paradoxical, difficult and highly worrying scenario of intrafamilial violence, where the young man, in order to return to his patrimony, must inevitably transgress the norms of the household he hopes to regain. The *Oresteia* demonstrates most strikingly how tragedy engages in a dialogue with the texts and models of the past to explore the problems, tensions and ambiguities within an accepted and traditional viewpoint. Aeschylus' Orestes, faced by his mother, asks what becomes the archetypal tragic question, the archetypal sign of doubt and confusion: 'What am I to do?' Homer's Orestes was an example of what one must do. Tragedy's ability to pose questions of its audience is displayed brilliantly in Aeschylus' rewriting of the narrative of Homer.

The second consequence of this shift of focus concerns the final scenes of the trilogy in particular. I have already discussed how the narrative of revenge and reversal ends up in the law-court in the centre of the city of Athens, and how the ending of the play depends not just on Orestes' acquittal but also on the Furies' acceptance of a new role in the city – an acceptance that leads to the final choruses of praise for the *polis* and its order. I have also discussed how this narrative of conflict is seen as a conflict between the genders, where in each case, unlike Homer's narrative, women aim directly at power and domination, and where, in each case, the gender conflict is seen as a conflict between obligations to the city and obligations to blood ties. What we can now see is that Aeschylus has rewritten Homer's narrative to give it a specifically political point. That is, to put it succinctly, whereas for Homer the answers to the conflicts of his narrative were to be located in the order of the *oikos*, for Aeschylus the answer is to be found in the *polis*.

I talked in the first chapter of this book of the importance of the *polis* as a frame for tragedy. Now we can see that this is certainly not just a sociological or historical 'background' to tragedy. The *polis* develops between Homer – where it does not exist in any recognizable fifth-century form – and the sixth century. The democratic *polis* is a new and rapidly changing culture in the fifth century. Aeschylus can be seen to be rewriting the privileged and paradigmatic stories of the past for the new context of the *polis*. The political focus of the *Oresteia*, then, develops not merely when the scene of the work shifts to Athens. From the opening lines of the trilogy the emphasis on gender opposition and on the conflicts of obligations is leading significantly towards the *polis* of Athens and its institutions. The transgressions, violence and revenge of the *Odyssey* can find resolution within the frame of the *oikos*. In Aeschylus' trilogy, the *oikos* itself needs to be relocated within the frame of the city. The rewriting of Homer in the *Oresteia* is no mere literary interplay. Aeschylus stages the problems of the old story before his city, here and now. In the process, he forges a new myth for the new culture of the democratic *polis*.

So, then, a charter for the *polis*? On the one hand, it is clear that the conclusion of the *Oresteia* in the centre of Athens itself is highly significant. The repetitive violence and blood-thirsty retribution stop; the opposition of male and female comes together in the patriarchal order of the *polis*. The importance of the *polis* itself can be seen in the way that Homer's epic finds a whole new frame and conclusion. So, in all these ways that I have discussed in the previous three sections of the chapter, the *Oresteia* can be said to have constructed a charter myth for the *polis* of Athens. Indeed, the final procession of the play, as the Furies are escorted to their new home in Athens, is staged in such a way as to recall the Athenian festival of the Great Panathenaia. The Great Panathenaia, as the name suggests, was a festival of all Athens. Its central celebration was a great procession to the Acropolis where a sacrifice was made to Athene. So, as Athene directs the final procession of the *Oresteia*, the play represents the city to the city, celebrating its goddess and itself as community. Certainly this is a significant and moving final image for the trilogy.

On the other hand, the ending of the *Oresteia* is conditional rather than utopian. That is, the *polis* is the condition of possibility of the good life, but the threat of transgression remains. The *dikē* of the city depends on the future actions of the citizens. Perhaps most significantly of all, even though the *Eumenides* ends with the lauding of social order, the trilogy's exploration and questioning of the language of social order are allowed to resound. The threat of competing obligations and the tensions and conflicts in the language of *dikē* haunt even the final torchlit procession. Aeschylus' vision remains a tragic one.

So the conclusion of the *Oresteia* may be said both to uplift, celebrate, praise, and yet to allow its questions, worries and doubts still to sound within the celebration. 'A charter for the city?', then – perhaps the question mark should remain.

The mortal coil

In the previous section of this chapter, I have looked at ways in which the narrative is organized to rethink a paradigmatic story of sex, violence and power for the new social and political conditions of the democratic *polis*. In this section, I want to consider some ways in which man's place within these social and political conditions is represented within the *Oresteia*. For this too is crucial to Aeschylus' tragic vision.

9 Language and control: the violence of persuasion

I want first to look at how the use of language becomes a theme of the *Oresteia*. As much as the language of *dikē* is central to the expression of conflict in the trilogy, so the use and dangers of language itself become an object of especial concern for Aeschylus.

To begin, it is worth commenting on some essential background. In the radical democracy of Athens, public speaking played a fundamental role. The Assembly's debates, the law-courts' cases, even the more informal political discussions of *agorá* or symposium depend on the performance of speakers. To succeed in public life required success in oratory. In the fifth century, language also becomes the object of an explosion of intellectual consideration – the rapid development of a range of disciplines from the philosophy of language to linguistics: Aeschylus is placed at the beginning of this movement. Above all, the practice and study of rhetoric were engaged in with an intense concern. Professional teachers and handbooks of rhetoric burgeoned, offering the young and wealthy a knowledge that promised success within the political sphere; and the public awareness of this professionalization of persuasive technique is equally burgeoning. Language and how people use it is a hot topic in the fifth century.

Now, the narrative of revenge and reversal in the *Oresteia* is turned to highlight the use of language. I have already mentioned how Clytemnestra takes to an extreme a common Greek worry about women and deception. It is now time to look at this in a little more detail. The central scene that demonstrates the power of her language is the so-called 'carpet scene', where Agamemnon's entrance to the palace is barred by Clytemnestra who has purple tapestries spread for him to walk on. She spins a speech of welcome that hypocritically recounts her despair at his absence and her joy at his return. She also recalls how many false reports of Agamemnon's death have disturbed her: as so often, a speech of deception talks about deceptive speeches. She invites him to enter the palace across the spread tapestries. Agamemnon, however, is quite clear that to walk on the tapestries is an unacceptable act. Such conspicuous consumption of the household property (Jones) is not the act of a Greek man (*Aga*. 918–25): 'Do not coddle me in womanish ways nor like a barbarian,' he says, 'respect me as a man, not a god.' Agamemnon clearly recognizes that to trample this finery would be a transgressive act, an act to be associated with the female or the barbarian (those defining negatives of citizenship), and an act to bring on him the wrath of the gods. When he does walk on the carpets, then, there is dramatized in a brilliant theatrical gesture the paradox of the victor as victim, the punisher as transgressor.

Agamemnon steps on to the carpets, however, because he has been persuaded by Clytemnestra. In a brief but dense dialogue, she attacks each of his reasons for not stepping on the tapestries, manipulates his responses, and, as he weaves her web of words, concludes significantly, 'Be persuaded! Yield your power (*kratos*) to me willingly.' What is dramatized here is the queen's persuasive language in the pursuit of dominance. Clytemnestra's power over the king, her ability to make him trample the finery of his house, displays the power of manipulative rhetoric at work.

The 'carpet scene', however, has been prepared for carefully in the preceding scenes of the *Agamemnon*. The first episode of the play is the so-called 'beacon speeches scene'. Here, the chorus questions Clytemnestra about the beacons that have appeared. In two lengthy speeches of great authority and impressiveness, she explains that Troy has fallen to the Greeks. In the first speech she describes the arrival of the beacon, its route from Troy to Argos. She recounts *how* it has travelled from place to place. After this speech, the chorus asks her to explain further, since they remain unconvinced; they would like to hear it again. In the second lengthy speech, Clytemnestra describes the sack of Troy. That is, she spins an account of the message of the beacon. After this speech, the chorus concludes with lines part of which I have already quoted: 'Woman, now you are speaking like a sensible man with understanding. I have heard your trustworthy proofs and I am prepared to address the gods in thanks.' There are three particular ways this remarkable episode looks forward to the 'carpet scene'. First, quite simply, it shows Clytemnestra persuading a group of men ('you speak like a man . . .') with manipulative and entrancing rhetoric. The chorus is made to believe what the queen wants it to believe. Secondly, the whole scene – the first episode of the trilogy – takes as its focus the arrival and meaning of a signal. Communication as a theme is highlighted from the start. (There is no suggestion of such a beacon chain in any earlier version of the story.) Thirdly and perhaps most interestingly, Clytemnestra's two speeches separate the signal and its meaning: the first speech talks about just the transmission of the beacon, the second about its possible significance. The fact that Clytemnestra cannot possibly know what happened at the sack of Troy – she weaves an imaginative account – emphasizes how signs and meanings can be separated – and manipulated. Clytemnestra's future manipulation of words and their meanings, or of the act of stepping on the tapestries and its meaning, is introduced in the 'beacon speeches scene', its discussion and manipulation of the process of signal-sending and reading.

The second episode of the play also revolves around messages, since it consists of the arrival of the messenger with news of the Greeks' imminent return; and his return to the king with a false message from Clytemnestra. When the messenger comes in, the chorus tries to hint that all is not well in the city, but the messenger quite fails to appreciate their veiled language. Indeed, when the chorus says dramatically that 'even death would be a great grace', the messenger replies, 'Yes! For things have gone well', as if they were expecting to die for joy at the prospect of the army's return. This misunderstanding stands as a significant prelude to the messenger's report, and his next commission: to take back to Agamemnon Clytemnestra's message, namely, that Agamemnon should hurry home to find his 'trustworthy wife in the house, as he left her, the noble watchdog of the home, enemy to his enemies . . .' (a message that prompts from the chorus a remark about the need for 'precise interpreters of speech'). So, in this scene too, communication is importantly dramatized as flawed, open to manipulation, dangerous and in need of careful interpretation.

The two episodes leading up to the 'carpet scene', then, both show us Clytemnestra manipulating the process of communication and suggest the danger inherent in her language. So, indeed, Clytemnestra, as she appears over the bodies of Agamemnon and Cassandra, boasts, 'I have said many things before to suit the occasion; now I will not be ashamed to say the opposite.' She is indeed, as the chorus expresses in amazement, 'so bold of tongue'. Shameless – 'I will not be ashamed' – in her language as in her sexual behaviour.

Between Agamemnon's entrance to the house and Clytemnestra's appearance over the bodies comes the Cassandra scene. Again communication as a theme is integral to the scene, since Cassandra is the prophetess whose gift from Apollo is always to tell the truth and never to be believed. The scene – the longest in the trilogy – is an extended dramatization of the failure of communication. It begins with Clytemnestra trying to persuade Cassandra into the house. Cassandra stands in silence. The chorus and Clytemnestra wonder whether the foreign princess can understand Greek, what sign language to use, can an interpreter be found . . . again the process of communication is expressly discussed as a significant prelude to the coming scene. When Clytemnestra returns in exasperation to the palace, Cassandra breaks into a cry that becomes articulate Greek. The silence, then, has been a meaningful gesture in the face of the manipulative language of the queen. It shows Cassandra's active disengagement from the queen. With the starkness of Aeschylus' characteristic architectural structuring, the play juxtaposes the woman who lies and persuades everyone to the woman who always tells the truth and persuades no one.

Cassandra's language of truth, however, is certainly not one of scientific clarity, as many people would think a true language should be. Rather, it is a heightened, metaphoric, allusive language of mantic insight (as Greek oracles typically are) (*Aga.* 1087–92):

Cassandra What house is this?
Chorus The house of the Atreidae. If you are not aware of this, I tell you, and this you will not say is false.
Cassandra No! Say rather it is a house god-hated, guilty within of kindred bloodshed, torture of its own, the shambles of men's butchery, the dripping floor.

Cassandra's simple question as to where she is being led gets a simple answer: 'the house of the Atreidae', and the chorus goes on to re-emphasize the process of communication with their strange periphrasis, 'If you are not aware of this, I tell you, and this you will not say is false' – their information is offered as true and informative and direct. Yet Cassandra cannot accept their reply. She corrects them – 'No! . . . rather' – and respecifies the house as a god-hated, self-consuming slaughterhouse. Cassandra's reply shows the significance of the chorus' apparently banal periphrasis. For she precisely does not accept their answer as truth, even if it is not enough simply to call it false. Cassandra's truth is constructed out of intertwined metaphors, an intense concentration of expression that suggests a unique access to the complexities of events, and a language capable of expressing such complexity.

Clytemnestra's persuasive force, then, is set against Cassandra's unpersuasive truth. An awareness of the dangers and powers of language is thus carefully fostered throughout the *Agamemnon*. This leads to many attempts to find control over language and its use through the trilogy. Perhaps the most important way this is seen is with prayers. Language is nowhere more binding than when addressing the gods. The wrong words produce the wrong result: lack of care can be disastrous. So, in the *Choephoroi*, Electra, before pouring her libation at the tomb of her father, worries at length about the correct words to use, and introduces the distinction between 'juror' and 'revenge bringer' that I discussed earlier, as she broaches the tricky question of what could be a pious prayer for the death of her mother. So, the chorus, as Aegisthus enters the palace, sings 'Zeus, Zeus what am I to say? From where can I begin as I pray and call on you? How am I to end after saying what is right?' The danger of words produces the need for an intense care with language.

Orestes, however, is expressly instructed by Apollo to kill Clytemnestra as she had killed, and indeed adopts a plan of deception: he arrives disguised as a messenger to gain entrance to the palace. The parallel with the *Agamemnon*'s scenes of message sending is clear. As he is about to enter the house, however, he adds another important element to the discussion. He hopes someone in authority will come to receive his message, 'a woman, but a man is more fitting. For shame in conversation makes words blear-eyed. But a man speaks out boldly to a man, and gives a clear indication of what he means' (*Cho.* 664–7). Orestes suggests that men and women cannot communicate clearly with one another – because of 'shame' in contact between the genders. Dramatically, this may raise an expectation that Aegisthus will appear, in order to increase the effect of the 'shameless' Clytemnestra's immediate arrival at the door. But it also serves to link the interest in communication with the concerns of gender conflict that I discussed earlier. Certainly Clytemnestra's speech of welcome to the false messenger that follows fulfils all of Orestes' worries. For she invites him into her house 'where there are fitting things: warm baths, beds to charm toil, and the presence of just expressions'. Not only is this house far from 'fitting', but also, since Agamemnon was killed in a 'warm bath', and since the 'bed' and its 'charms' were the source of her corruption, and since hypocritically 'just expressions' led Agamemnon to his death, there is considerable irony – 'blear-eyed words' – in this exchange between woman and man. Each conflict of the trilogy is depicted as a clash between the genders; communication between male and female is dramatized as ironic, deceptive, and aiming at dominance.

The law-court of the *Eumenides* transforms the violence of revenge into the conflict of speeches. The establishment and rule of law, which formalizes and consecrates social relations of order, highlight the necessary involvement of ideology in the use of language in a social setting: the decision of the court, as we have seen, depends in part at least on the socio-political position of Agamemnon and Clytemnestra as male and female. Yet the law-court also leads to Athene's persuasion of the Furies. The trilogy ends with another scene of manipulative language at work. Where in the *Agamemnon* the chorus had sung 'god's grace is violent', now Athene says that there is no need for Zeus's force – the thunderbolt: persuasion will deflect the threat of their curses (*Eum.* 826–31). Indeed, Athene rejoices (*Eum.* 970) 'that the eyes of Persuasion were watching over my tongue and mouth. Zeus of the meeting place (*agorá*) has triumphed.' The final reconciliation of the trilogy, then, is effected by the force of persuasion through which the plot of revenge progressed. Language has been the means and matter of transgression: it becomes the means and matter of reconciliation, as the chorus is persuaded to turn from curse to blessing.

So, the trilogy moves from the signal of the beacons to the process of law: the *Oresteia* charts the social functioning of language in the *polis*. This theme of the use of language is an important element in placing man within the social frame I discussed earlier. Language, when used rightly in prayer, blessing, curse and naming, can have a directive and binding effect. In law it provides the institutional means of mediating the conflicts of violence. Yet the fear of the misuse of language remains in direct proportion to its power. Persuasion – manipulative rhetoric – can be used to forward the disruption and disorder that repeatedly racks the house of Agamemnon. Persuasion is central to the Assembly and law-courts of democratic Athens. Aeschylus in the democratic institution of the theatre dramatizes the dangers of persuasion at work, and shows how the corruption of the processes of communication leads to violence and disorder – and is a sign of violence and disorder. The instability of a word like *dikē*, then, must also be seen as part of the incertitude of human communication. It is basic to Aeschylus' tragic vision of things that the precariousness of human existence is necessarily tied to the precariousness of language.

10 Prophecy, fear and the influence of the past

The fear of the misuse of language is only one aspect of a pervasive feeling of terror and mistrust that runs through the *Oresteia*. The first long ode of the *Agamemnon* has a repeated refrain 'Sing woe, woe, but let the good prevail', and this mixture of worry and hope remains until the last scenes of the trilogy. The chorus of elders sings, as Agamemnon enters the palace (*Aga.* 975–83): 'Why does this dread feeling constantly fly, a guardian of my prophetic heart? Unbidden, unpaid, the song plays the seer; I cannot spurn it, like obscure dreams, nor let persuasive security settle the seat of my mind.' This lurking dread, a terror that predicts future disaster and prevents security, sums up the bleak atmosphere of much of the work. Indeed, even when Athene establishes the Areopagus in the *Eumenides*, she says that fear holds a crucial place in her city, fear prevents the crimes of citizens.

This terror, particularly the fear of what is going to happen, leads to a series of attempts to gain control over the passage of events. One of the commonest ways of seeking for this control is suggested in the language of the chorus quoted above, namely, prophecy – the art of the seer. The Cassandra scene is the longest scene of prophecy in Greek tragedy, but this is only one of many moments of foretelling in the *Oresteia*. Clytemnestra's dream in the *Choephoroi*, for example, causes terror because it is seen as prophetic. The libations for the dead Agamemnon are an attempt to control the implications of the dream through ritual; but not only are the libations redirected by Electra, but also the dream itself is given its authoritative interpretation by Orestes. Clytemnestra dreamt she gave birth to a snake, which drew blood from her breast when put to nurse. Orestes prays and declares that the dream is accurately prophetic: for, he says, since the snake came from where he did and suckled where he did, the dream means that Clytemnestra, since she has nourished a monster, must die violently: 'I turned consummate snake shall kill her. So the dream declares.' This interpretative gesture shows the power and danger of prophecy. On the one hand, the dream is seen as a binding indication of the future: Clytemnestra is to die violently at the hands of Orestes. On the other hand, the language in which the prophecy is expressed has more worrying implications also. Orestes declares himself a monster, a snake, an agent of violence – all words that resonate with other moments of intrafamilial violence in the house of Agamemnon. The prophecy, as it foretells the matricide, also binds Orestes into the narrative of the family curse.

It is a prophecy from an omen that sets up the first tragic conflict described in the *Agamemnon*. At Aulis, the expedition is sent on its way by an omen, two eagles, 'the king of birds appearing to the kings of the fleet', who kill a pregnant hare (*Aga*. 111–20). This is interpreted by Calchas, the seer of the Greeks, to mean that Troy will fall; but he adds the gloss that he also hopes it does not mean that some hatred of the gods will cloud the expedition, because Artemis hates the meal of the eagles. He prays to Apollo to prevent the goddess from demanding another sacrifice – a sacrifice which will indeed, as we have seen, take place, and foster the tragic conflicts of the house of Agamemnon. There are two crucial points that need to be made here about this complex passage. The first is to note a similar pattern shared by this prophecy and Orestes' dream analysis. Calchas' prophecy from the omen is indeed a foretelling – Troy will fall, another sacrifice will be demanded – but the language of the omen and its interpretation is dense with implications. For example, the eagles are said not just to kill the hare but to 'sacrifice' it – and this leads to the idea of 'another sacrifice' and Iphigeneia's death. (I will discuss the wording of this interpretation later in sections 11 and 13.) Secondly, the pattern of cause and effect that this omen establishes is highly difficult. In other versions of Agamemnon at Aulis, the sacrifice of Iphigeneia is demanded because of a crime by Agamemnon. In one version, he kills a stag in a sacred grove of Artemis where it is illegal to slaughter; in another, he kills a stag and boasts that he is a better hunter than Artemis, for which the goddess punishes him. In both cases, there is a simple pattern of transgression against the divine figure and punishment by her. In Aeschylus' version, however, the sacrifice is demanded by the goddess because of her hatred of an omen – the eagle's meal. How does this lead to Agamemnon's requirement of sacrificing his daughter? Critics have argued at length on the issue, but it seems that this obfuscation of a clear pattern of cause and effect is typical of Aeschylus' highly intricate and difficult view of the connection between events – where human ignorance and uncertainty necessarily feature, as do the contrasting power and control of the divine.

So, as much as an omen gives a binding signal of the future, *how* such omens and prophecies relate to events is the subject of doubt, confusion and the uncertainty of interpretation. The many scenes of prophecy in the *Oresteia*, then, testify both to the search for certain control over what is to happen and to the inevitable instability of that control for humans over the passage of events.

The inability to make the gestures of foretelling with certainty is depicted as leading to an inability to act. When the death cries of Agamemnon are heard, the chorus of elders in an extraordinary dialogue wonders what is happening, and fails to do anything. There is a convention that the chorus does not enter the stage space of the actors, a convention which would normally prevent the chorus from, say, entering the palace and trying to stop the murder of the king. But this dialogue is written to tie in with the *Oresteia*'s interest in prophecy and control (*Aga.* 1366–9): 'By the evidence of the groans are we to prophesy that a man has died?' 'We must know clearly to discuss it. For guessing is quite different from clear knowledge.' Lack of knowledge – an inability to prophesy accurately from the evidence – leads to an incapacity for action.

Yet what of Cassandra, the one human figure in the trilogy who does have perfect knowledge of the future? In a dramatic gesture, she throws away her prophet's staff and garland, as she progresses to her death. 'There is', she says (*Aga.* 1299), 'no escaping it, friends, not any longer.' Cassandra's fate is inescapable. An absolute knowledge of the future means an absolutely determined world. Where the chorus hoped that clear knowledge and prediction would bring control and mastery over events, Cassandra shows that certain knowledge brings merely a heightened sense of an unavoidable doom.

The sense of human action that Aeschylus constructs here is not a happy one. Doubt and ignorance about the future lead to a search for control through prophecy and omens, and to a pervasive feeling of terror; but the omens and prophecies turn out to be not merely binding and predictive but also full of hidden implications. What is more, the one human figure who does have a certain vision of the future progresses to her death 'like an ox to the altar'.

If the passage of events produces a sense of the lack of human control, what of the past? How does the past affect human action in the world of the *Oresteia*? I have already mentioned on several occasions how the narrative of violence in Agamemnon's family stretches into the past and how Cassandra in particular tells of the history of destruction between men and women, parents and children. It is clear that this past is seen as a *determining* factor in events. When Calchas explains the omen of the eagles, his final remarks point to the continuing curse that haunts the family as a *cause* of Agamemnon's tragic situation. Orestes' double bind too is the product of the continuing effects of his parents' actions.

There are two models that are repeatedly used for this effect of the past on the present. The first is the return of a parent's characteristics in the child. Perhaps the best example of this is the famous parable told in the choral ode after the messenger scene in the *Agamemnon*, which tells the story of a lion-cub. A man took a lion-cub 'unweaned and loving the teat' into his home, and as a cub it was gentle, kind to his children and pleasant. The household played with it like a baby, and the lion, constrained by the needs of its belly, fawned. 'But matured by time it displayed the character it had from its parents; for in return for its rearing, unbidden it feasted in wild destructive slaughter of the flocks and the household was mired with gore' (*Aga.* 727–32). The lion appears gentle, but over the passage of time it inevitably shows the nature it has inherited from its parents, and destruction results, the violent bloodying of the *oikos*. This parable is told in the first instance as an illustration of the misplaced joy of the Trojans at the arrival of the beautiful Helen. But the imagery of lions, bloody destruction in the house, and the characteristics of parents resurfacing in the child are repeatedly used of each of the characters of the trilogy, so that the image of 'the lion in the house' becomes applicable to the whole narrative (Knox). So, for example, Cassandra calls Clytemnestra a 'lioness' and Aegisthus a 'weakling lion', and Agamemnon a 'noble lion' – as each reveals a propensity for violence. We have already seen how Orestes repays his rearing at the breast in blood: the chorus sings as he and Clytemnestra enter the palace (*Cho.* 937–8): 'the double lion has entered the house of Agamemnon . . .' The Furies in their pursuit of Orestes are declared by Apollo to be more suited to 'the cave of a blood-supping lion' – as they threaten to continue the violence within the home. The 'lion in the house' thus becomes a parable for the inescapable effects of parental inheritance – the determining force of the past on the present.

The second model that is repeatedly used for this relation of past and present is that of childbirth. In the same ode that includes the lion in the house parable, the chorus sings (*Aga.* 751–5) of another ancient proverb, that 'great wealth when it reaches fullness begets and does not die childless; from good fortune flourishes insatiable despair for the race'. This generalization echoes a standard idea of Greek moral writing, that wealth leads to excess which leads to the arrogant violence called *hubris*. The chorus goes on to say that they disagree with this notion because, in their view, it is 'the impious action that gives birth to more, like to it in generation', and they conclude (*Aga.* 763–5): 'old violence [*hubris*] loves to give birth to new violence [*hubris*] amid the evils of men'. The chorus may distinguish their own opinion that it is wrong that leads to wrong from the common idea that wealth produces its own tendencies to transgression, but throughout their reflections there is a continuous vocabulary of childbirth and generation: wealth 'begets', does not die 'childless', impious action 'gives birth', *hubris* 'gives birth'. As the lion in the house reproduces parental characteristics, so the narrative of cause and effect is expressed as the action of birthing and generation.

The past, then, plays a determining role in the present, and the ways in which this relation is expressed link the specific history of intrafamilial violence in Agamemnon's household to a more general pattern of behaviour through the shared language of child/parent relations. This leads to a remarkable overlap of expression as Orestes is about to knock on the palace door. The chorus sings that the Fury 'leads back into the house the child of former bloodshed to pay in time for the pollution', or 'leads back into the house this child to pay in time for the pollution of former bloodshed'. The Greek syntax is strictly ambiguous. On the first reading, Orestes' return is seen as the latest crime in the history of crimes: his action is the 'child of former bloodshed'. On the second understanding, Orestes is 'the child' who is being brought home to avenge his mother's past acts of violence. The two senses of 'child' interfuse, as the familial narrative of Orestes overlaps with the general pattern of the repeated violence of revenge.

It is striking that even at the end of the trilogy this tragic sense of a man being mired in an existence determined by a past over which he has no control remains strongly present. After the Furies accept Athene's proposals and start to sing blessings on Athens, the goddess sings of the relations between humans and the Furies as punishers of human transgression in her new dispensation. A man who comes into contact with the Furies 'does not know from where the blows of life come. For the sins of former generations lead him to the Furies, and silent destruction wastes him, shout loud as he may, in hating rage' (*Eum.* 933–7). The goddess here authorizes inevitable human ignorance – man does not know where the disasters he experiences in life come from. The reason is that the errors of former generations require punishment even in the future. There is no explanation for such punishment – doom is silent, for all a man may shout. This grim picture of a human's lack of control over the passage of events forms a haunting bleakness amid the lauding of the *polis* as social order.

Throughout the *Oresteia*, then, the passage of events creates fear and a sense of doubt as the shifting patterns of cause and effect elude man's attempts at mastery. It is a central and tragic tension of the *Oresteia* that as the narrative moves towards the celebration of the *polis*, the picture of individual humans' lives, mired in ignorance, caught in familial narratives, and punished by a silent, unremitting and inexplicable doom, remains constant.

11 The imagery of order

In my discussion of 'the lion in the house' parable, I pointed out how each of the major characters of the trilogy becomes associated with the imagery of the parable. This is typical of Aeschylus' writing, not merely for the ambiguity and continuing significance with which the parable becomes invested, but also for the extended pattern of imagery, growing and deepening over the length of the work (Lebeck). For, criss-crossing the trilogy, is a series of interrelated systems of imagery that develop with the narrative. In this section, I shall look at some of this imagery that is closely connected with man's place in the order of things.

I wish to begin with the imagery of sacrifice and first with some necessary background on the rite itself in Greek culture. Sacrifice is an absolutely fundamental part of Greek religion. It involves the ritualized killing and consumption of a domestic animal by a delimited group of people, who constitute a group through shared participation in the ritual. This group killing of an animal has been analysed by some historians of religion as a ritualized way of mediating violence within a community by directing it towards another object – a 'scapegoat', as it were (Burkert, Girard); but for my present purposes I am most concerned with the way that sacrifice is used to express a sense of a human community's attitudes and values. First, sacrifice establishes a hierarchical system of 'worlds' – that is, sacrifice institutionalizes the human community in opposition to the divine world (which receives the sacrifice) and the animal world (which provides the sacrificial victim) (Detienne and Vernant). It further distinguishes between wild animals that are hunted (e.g. boars) and domestic animals that are sacrificed (e.g. pigs); and between humans who form the community and humans who are excluded. (When Orestes wishes to prove to Athene that he has been properly purified, he asserts he has taken part in sacrifices in different communities – that is, he has been treated as an acceptable member of human society rather than as a polluted outcast.) Sacrifice, thus, expresses man's place in the order of things: distinct from the wild and domestic world of the beasts and from the immortal sphere of the divine. Secondly, sacrifice encodes a set of values about human culture and nature. For example, the animal sacrificed is a domestic animal, part of man's dominance over nature; the animal is sprinkled with corn, the product of human agriculture, and wine, the product of human viticulture. Men eat the animal's flesh; the bones are burnt to the gods, who enjoy only the savour of the roasting. Man's necessary relation to the land in agriculture for the production of food, and man's necessary cooking of food are thus contrasted with the wild animal's raw consumption of flesh, and the gods' requirement of only the smoke and smell of the sacrifice. Thus, sacrifice encodes ideas about human corporeality, food production and labour. Thirdly, sacrifice as ritual with its taboos and careful observance of rules forms a controlled institution of bloodshed (to set next to hunting and warfare, and to contrast, say, with the violence of revenge) and, in the final feast, a social occasion for the celebration of the group.

It is clear, then, that the proper performance of sacrifice is in a variety of ways a fundamental expression of man's place in the order of things. In the *Oresteia*, if there is one image that provides a store of imagery to be recalled throughout the trilogy, it is the sacrifice of Iphigeneia. It colours all the acts of violence in the work. The sacrifice of Iphigeneia is, however, a corrupt sacrifice (Zeitlin). She is taken 'like a goat', a human rather than an animal. She is sacrificed by her father. In sacrificial ritual there is a 'comedy of innocence' designed to prove that the animal wishes to be sacrificed: by throwing some water on the head of the animal and then sprinkling it with groats of corn the animal is made to nod acceptance of the rite. Iphigeneia, however, is held on the altar by force, her mouth is gagged lest she say anything ill-omened. There is no feast that follows, but rather the chorus recalls how in the palace previously the daughter had sung at her father's table at such celebrations. The sacrifice of Iphigeneia embodies exactly what Calchas the prophet had feared (*Aga.* 150–1): 'another sacrifice, lawless, feastless, inborn creator of strife, that fears no man'. Iphigeneia's sacrifice precisely inverts the proper practice of the ritual.

The fighting around Troy, however, is also described as a 'preliminary sacrifice' (*Aga.* 65) to the city's destruction, and the eagles killing the pregnant hare, as we have seen, are said (*Aga.* 136) to 'sacrifice' their victim. Clytemnestra, as ever, takes this language to an extreme, particularly in her triumphant speech over the dead bodies, where she describes her three lethal blows against Agamemnon as pouring three libations – the usual ritual number – and delights in the spilling of blood in a sexually charged perversion of ritual behaviour. She also invites Cassandra into the house 'to share in the sacrifice' (*Aga.* 1037), as 'the victim is by the altar' (*Aga.* 1056) – a heavily ironic welcome, since it is as victim that Cassandra is to participate in this sacrifice. Cassandra too sees herself entering the house as a sacrificial victim; it is thus with great irony that when Cassandra balks at the door because (*Aga.* 1309–10) 'the house breathes blood dripping gore', the chorus banally responds 'Nay, this is the smell of the sacrifices at the hearth.' The central scene of the play, then, is also represented as a perverted sacrificial killing. The lion-cub too is described when young as being 'in the preliminary sacrifice of life' (*Aga.* 720), and when it kills, it is termed 'the sacrificing priest of destruction' (*Aga.* 735). Even the killing of Thyestes' children is called a sacrificial slaughter (*Aga.* 1036–7). In brief, there are seven acts of killing in the *Agamemnon*, and they are all pictured as a ritual, a corrupt sacrifice.

In the *Choephoroi*, however, it is at first sight surprising that the killing of Clytemnestra is not described in sacrificial language. Orestes claims the Fury of the house is drinking 'a third draught' – lines which recall Clytemnestra's violent perversion of the three libations – but otherwise the motif of the corrupted sacrifice does not appear. In part, this accords with the positive ritual performances that dominate the first part of the play. In part, it must be seen as one of the factors of asymmetry between Orestes' killing of his mother and her killing of Agamemnon – an asymmetry leading towards the trial's decision as enforcement of the asymmetry of gender roles in Greek culture. Orestes, for all the other paradoxes of his position, is not depicted as a corrupt sacrificer.

The *Eumenides*, however, shows a marked revival of the imagery of sacrifice. The Furies themselves see Orestes as a sacrificial victim throughout the binding song, and threaten to suck his blood from his living marrow in a monstrous perversion of the ordered killing of sacrifice. Again, a human object of sacrifice; but now with divine figures as sacrificers. The Furies threaten a corrupt form of killing.

There is, then, a pattern to the imagery of sacrifice and a repeated point. It expresses the violence of reciprocal revenge as a corruption of a wider system of norms, a wider sense of man's place. By depicting each act of killing as a sacrifice, Aeschylus constructs each killing as a sign and symptom of disorder within the community and its norms. So there is considerable significance in the fact that in the final scene of the trilogy the Furies become the receivers of sacrifice from humans as honoured divinities (*Eum.* 1037). As the order of the *polis* is celebrated, there is a return to the proper ritual performance of sacrifice as part of that order. The imagery of sacrifice can be called 'teleological', that is, imagery that is inherently structured towards a particular end point (or *telos*), namely, the proper relations of man, beasts and gods in the *dikē* of the *polis*.

There are other systems of imagery that work in a similarly teleological way. Hunting, for example, is an institution in Greek culture that involves much more than exercise and the killing of animals for sport. It is another group activity, in this case exclusively male, that helps define the group. It helps define the group not only in the sense that the first hunt can be seen as an initiation into the body of male adults, but also in the way that hunting, like sacrifice, helps define man's position with regard to the natural world. Hunting takes place in the wild; the men leave the city and enter a special space outside the city, thus defining the boundaries of the civilized space. The men hunt only wild animals, and thus hunting and sacrifice together help articulate the divisions of the natural world from the point of view of the cultural world of the *polis*. Hunting is also a shared, controlled, ritualized form of killing, which, like sacrifice, produces meat for a group feast, group celebration.

It is perhaps not surprising that hunting is an image that becomes closely connected with the narrative of revenge and reversal. The imagery is used first of the Greek expedition to Troy, which 'hunts down the city' and follows the tracks to Troy like hunters. Cassandra is said to sniff out slaughter like a hunting dog – and both Cassandra and Clytemnestra see the killing of Agamemnon as the setting of traps and nets for the king, imagery that becomes dramatically staged in the robe in which the king is enveloped in the bath. The hunter, however, becomes the hunted: Orestes, as if a young man being initiated into the world of adult males (Vernant and Vidal-Naquet), hunts out Clytemnestra and displays her hunting weapons with her dead body. In his turn, he becomes hunted as 'the dogs of his mother' pursue him. Indeed, in the *Eumenides*, the Furies are first represented groaning in sleep like a dog, and from the groans gradually is articulated the hunter's cry, 'Catch him, catch him, catch him' (*Eum.* 130). The Furies follow the trace of blood to Athens, like hunting dogs, and seek there 'the cowering animal' (*Eum.* 252). The same term is used of Orestes that is used of the pregnant hare, killed by the eagles, in the opening ode of the trilogy – as the logic of the narrative of reversal images the hunter Orestes now as the victim animal, and connects his situation back to the other hunted and destroyed figures of the trilogy.

Yet as the Furies become part of the city, this language also changes. Whereas in the pursuit of revenge they proclaimed in an extraordinary image (*Eum*. 253), 'The smell of human blood laughs at me', in their blessing of the city they pray (*Eum*. 980–3) that 'the dust does not drink the black blood of citizens, and through passion for revenge, embrace the city's ruin in slaughters in return'. The Furies pray here for the absence of the very force they have embodied in the play. As the imagery of corrupt sacrifice and corrupt hunting has been used to express the violence of revenge, so the final blessings of the Furies take on a specific significance as the reordering of that corruption.

Both sacrifice and hunting articulate man's place in and against the natural world, and as such these systems of imagery interlock in interesting ways with the pervasive animal imagery of the drama, and with the imagery of agriculture and the natural forces of wind and rain and sun. These networks of imagery can be said to be inherently value-laden in that sacrifice, hunting, agriculture imply a proper place for man and a proper behaviour for man. These networks of imagery, however, are also 'teleological' in the *narrative*, that is, they are constructed to move from a sense of disorder or corruption to an end point in the order of the *polis*. This imagery thus becomes a key way of linking the narrative's movement to a sense of man's place within the structure of things.

Yet in typically Aeschylean fashion this structuring is self-consciously complicated by a thematic focus on 'endings' themselves, particularly with regard to the Greek word *telos* (whence 'teleological'). Character after character hopes for 'the end', aims at 'the end', declares 'the end' has come, only to find it to have been another link in the chain of events. It is this in part that creates the sense of vendetta as, precisely, never ending. So, for example, the chorus of the *Choephoroi* hopes that Clytemnestra's death is the third and last storm to rock the house (*Cho*. 1067): 'the third storm has ended [*tel*-]' (Clay). Orestes, however, had said (*Cho*. 1021), 'I do not know where the *telos* will be', and is sent to await

(*Eum.* 143) 'the *telos* of *dikē*'. When the lion-cub has reached maturity, it is said to have reached a *telos* (*Aga.* 727); the analysis of the dream by Orestes searches for its *telos* (*Cho.* 528). There are many other such examples. But what is especially important is the ambiguity of the term *telos* itself. I have translated it 'end' or 'final point'. It also implies 'consummation'; the 'end' that is death; the 'consummation of a religious rite', most commonly sacrifice – thus linking the imagery of ending and the imagery of sacrifice; it also means 'that which is paid', 'a tax' – and all these senses of *telos* can be seen highlighted in the *Oresteia*. Indeed, the term is used in many of the work's most charged moments precisely for this ambiguous range of sense. For example, as Agamemnon enters the palace in the *Agamemnon*, Clytemnestra prays (*Aga.* 972–3) to 'Zeus Teleios' to 'fulfil' [*tel*-] her prayers and 'may it concern you to fulfil [*tel*-] what you intend'. Now, although 'fulfil my prayer' may appear a standard request of a god, especially Zeus Teleios ('the fulfiller'), it is also Agamemnon's death (*telos*) that is being requested, a death repeatedly represented as a sacrifice (*telos*). So, in the previous line (971), Clytemnestra has called her husband *teleios*, 'perfect', 'fulfilled' – a term used traditionally of the victim of a sacrifice. Now is also the fulfilment (*telos*) of Clytemnestra's plot, and Agamemnon's payment (*telos*) for his past crimes. Clytemnestra's deceptive rhetoric here manipulates the utterance of a prayer to allow her design frighteningly to appear in the ambiguous language of *telos*. So, when Orestes awaits 'the *telos* of *dikē*' (*Eum.* 243), the two Greek terms together suggest a range of possible meanings: 'my fulfilment through justice'; 'the end point of the law-court'; 'my death as punishment'. The ambiguity is significant at this turning point of the narrative in that it suggests the set of possible outcomes of Orestes' arrival in Athens.

There is, then, a certain open-endedness about the language of fulfilment and ending in the *Oresteia*. Aeschylus thus conjoins the imagery of order that I have been discussing with a sense of the instability of 'final points', an uncertainty about endings as moments of control for humans. As much as the imagery of order suggests a sense of man's proper place, the imagery of false endings and the ambiguity of the language of ending together serve to surround the notion of fulfilment with uncertainty and the doubt we have seen to be central to Aeschylus' representation of human control.

12　The divine frame

The first word of the *Odyssey*, as we saw, is 'man'. The first word of the *Oresteia* is 'gods', as the watchman prays for 'release from toil'. The last words of the *Oresteia* invite song as 'Zeus all-seeing and the Fates thus come down together'. The divine frame of the trilogy is fundamental to Aeschylus' work (as it is to all Greek tragedy). The trilogy has repeated prayers, religious rituals, and, in the *Eumenides*, the appearance of the gods themselves in the courtroom drama. Characters reflect on the involvement of divinities in human action; choral odes widen the discussion to the most general sphere; individual gods are invoked for help at specific moments. At all levels of writing, Aeschylus' work is informed by the divine.

This divine world is not limited to the twelve Olympian gods headed by Zeus. It also includes figures like the Furies, the Sun, Night and other more abstract figures such as *Dikē* herself, as well as monsters, shadowy demons and giants. To talk of 'the gods' inevitably oversimplifies the complexity of a polytheistic system. The range of relations between humans and the divine, and between divine figures themselves, is remarkably variegated, and it is this that I wish to discuss briefly in this section.

We have already seen some relevant aspects of the background to this discussion in the previous sections of this book. We have seen how religion plays an integral role in the life of the *polis* that cannot properly be separated out as a particular sphere of concern. The many cults of the *polis* with their temples or shrines, sacrifices and other rituals, are part of most aspects of a citizen's life (from war to homelife, from theatre to the Assembly). The Athenian civic calendar had 144 days of festivals (though not all Athenians were expected to celebrate all of them)! Although many aspects of this cultic activity can properly be termed conservative, both in the sense that some basic practice remained unchanged over many years, and in the sense that such activity helps maintain a status quo, it would be wrong to think of Greek religion as 'orthodox' or doctrinaire in a modern sense. There was, for example, no fixed body of religious texts, no priestly caste, few elaborate rules of daily behaviour. What is more, new cults were often easily assimilated into the system, new temples dedicated. And with the growth of the *polis*, there were also

innumerable shifts of practice and ideology. Indeed, the fifth-century
enlightenment also focused its critical attention on the divine, and
many writers both discussed at length issues raised by the city's
theological apparatus, and by their discussions helped to change
attitudes to it and supported alternatives to it.

We have also seen how 'the tragic moment' – the social and intellectual conditions in which tragedy arises – can be seen to depend on
a clash of expectations concerning the divine (as the direct involvement of the divine in human action depicted in Homer stands in
tension with the sense of human responsibility and accountability
demanded by the legal and political system). It is first on this sense
of causality and the divine that I wish to offer some comments here.

The gods' involvement in the narrative of revenge is repeatedly
asserted. In the *Agamemnon*, the expedition to Troy is said to be 'sent
by Zeus' (*Aga.* 61–2); so too the omen of the eagles is said to 'send
the army', and since these are Zeus's birds, the assumption is easy
to make that the omen too comes from the gods. Artemis delays the
expedition; and Agamemnon is to kill his daughter to conform to
the instructions of the divine. When the report of Troy's fall comes,
the chorus immediately sees the hand of Zeus in it (*Aga.* 361–7),
just as the messenger (*Aga.* 525–6) sees the city's fall as the work of
'Zeus who brings *dikē*'. The storm that shatters the Greek fleet takes
place because the Greeks have desecrated the altars of Troy, and
Agamemnon's first words, as we have seen, are directed towards the
gods. Cassandra's fate of telling the truth and not being believed is
the result of her breaking faith with Apollo, and Apollo's possession
of her. Clytemnestra sees herself as the agent of divine forces in killing
Agamemnon.

In the *Choephoroi*, Orestes and Electra open with prayers to
Hermes; Orestes explains how Apollo is a direct controlling force
for his action; Pylades claims that all men must be counted enemy
before the oracles of the gods can be discounted (*Cho.* 900–2). The
revenge is seen to take place under the aegis and motivation of the
divine (*Cho.* 940–1). As the Furies appear to Orestes, an appeal is
made to Apollo, and in the *Eumenides*, the play opens in the house
of the god, and the gods, of course, take part in the action to such a
degree that when Orestes leaves the stage there is still one third of
the divine drama to run.

It is perhaps not surprising, then, in the light of this direct and constant involvement of divine forces in human action, that critics have often declared that this trilogy represents human action as controlled and determined by divine authority. As Homer's *Iliad* unfolds 'the plan of Zeus', so, it is claimed, the *Oresteia*'s double binds and resolutions depend on the plan of Zeus. This view is often combined with the notion that Aeschylus' theology and politics are deeply conservative – and so, for example, the deeply conservative critic Denys Page states that Aeschylus 'takes for granted certain long-established opinions about man's relation to the supernatural world; and he is not concerned to criticize doctrines which Solon [a political figure of the sixth century] in his time would have thought conventional'. So in Page's view Aeschylus' 'morality is simple and practical' and can be summed up as 'The will of Zeus be done . . . [man's] part is to obey.' We have already seen enough of the intricate and complex sense of human action, the connection between events and the tragic sense of competing obligations to make such an oversimplified view seem grossly distorting. Yet what place remains for human motivation, human choice, human control in such a god-ordered narrative?

The first thing to note is that, at many points of the narrative where the assertion of a controlling influence of a deity is made, critics like Page have been all too quick to ignore the rhetoric of explanation at work. So, for example, that the destruction of Troy is the work of Zeus – an echo of the Iliadic 'plan of Zeus' – is expressed by the chorus as follows (*Aga.* 367–72): 'They can say it is the blow of Zeus; this much can be traced in full. He has done what he has fulfilled. Men have said the gods do not think it right to care about humans who trample on the finery of things that should not be touched. But that is impious.' The Trojans can recognize the violence of Zeus; that much at least, claims the chorus, is clear. This implies first of all that there are other elements that are not included in this explanation – hidden, obscure or partial causes. Yet they follow this attempt at explanation with a bold, even tautological summation – 'he has done what he has fulfilled' – which is immediately framed by an alternative view of the question, which, they claim, is impious, namely, that the gods are not concerned with human transgression. (And note how the description of human transgression – 'trample on the finery of things that should not be touched' – looks forward to the 'carpet scene'.) The chorus, in other words, is struggling to understand the destruction of Troy in terms of human and divine activity, and they are constructing an argument, not merely stating how things are. The gods as figures become part of humans' attempts at comprehending things. So, in one of the most famous passages of reflection from the choral odes of the *Agamemnon*, the so-called 'Zeus hymn' (*Aga.* 160–83), the chorus indeed proposes that it is only Zeus who can cast the burden from a mind with accuracy, only the supporter of Zeus to whom wisdom comes – Zeus who has made it a fixed rule that knowledge comes from experience and that even the unwilling learn through the 'violent grace' of the divine. The chorus does indeed thus place Zeus as the supreme figure of authority who can offer humans sense – albeit through compulsion. Yet this passage comes between Calchas' reading of the omen of the hare and the eagles, and the playing out of Calchas' fear in Agamemnon's dilemma at Aulis. There has been no description of the delay at Aulis: the portrayal of Zeus has taken its place. Agamemnon's case is offered as an example of what the chorus has described as the power of Zeus. But how does it function as an example of violent grace? Of 'wisdom through experience'? Of the 'supporter of Zeus'? The 'Zeus hymn' both sets up Zeus as a transcendent authority and at the same time leaves the connections between that authority and the human action frightening, forceful and, in the specifics of Agamemnon's case, deeply obscure. Again, we see the chorus struggling towards a comprehension of events through the figuration of the divine. What humans know remains partial: 'this much at least . . .'

Divine authority and control, however, play a role not merely in humans' attempts to comprehend events, but also, more precisely, in humans' competing explanations which structure the tragic *agon*. This is nowhere clearer than in the debate between the chorus and the queen after Clytemnestra has appeared over the bodies of Agamemnon and Cassandra. Clytemnestra displays the bodies as 'the work of this my right hand, worker of justice' (*Aga.* 1405–6); she then swears (*Aga.* 1432–3) that she has slaughtered them 'by/with/for Justice, Destruction and The Fury of Revenge'; she then claims (*Aga.* 1476–9) that 'the thrice-fattened demon of the race' has been the cause of her action; finally, she asserts

(*Aga.* 1497–1503), 'You claim this is my work, that I am Agamemnon's wife; but appearing in the shape of the wife of the dead man, the ancient violent spirit of vengeance takes revenge for the transgressions of Atreus.' As Clytemnestra moves from claiming that this is 'the work of this my right hand' to 'this is the work of the ancient demon of the house', the chorus too shifts position. It is they who see the murder as the result of Helen's adultery (*Aga.* 1448–61); they blame the 'demon who falls on the house' (*Aga.* 1468) – a suggestion with which Clytemnestra agrees. They then sing, however (*Aga.* 1485–8), 'Woe, woe, through Zeus all-responsible, all-doing. For what is fulfilled (*tel-*) by men without Zeus? What of this is not god-determined?'. Not only do they propose omnipotent Zeus as the direct cause and agent of all things, but also there is in the Greek an etymological play between 'through' (*diai*) and 'Zeus' (*Dios*), which suggests a natural link between Zeus and agency. Here, the chorus seems to declare that events are indeed all the plan of Zeus, 'god-determined'. Yet in their very next speech (in response to Clytemnestra's claim that it was the demon in woman's shape who killed the king) the chorus asks 'Who will bear witness that you are not responsible for this slaughter?' The word 'not responsible', *anaitios*, directly echoes the description of Zeus as 'all-responsible', *panaitios* – and points neatly to the paradox. If Zeus is 'all-responsible', is Clytemnestra then 'not responsible'? The response to the central act of regicide *debates* the involvement of men and gods in the event, sets up different ways of comprehending the killing, different ways of attributing causal factors. It is not enough, then, to say simply that what is enacted is the 'plan of Zeus'. There is a far more complex rhetoric of explanation, doubt and contest at work here.

The same vocabulary of responsibility and cause occurs in the *Eumenides*. When the Furies first address Apollo directly they say (*Eum.* 199–200), 'You yourself are not in part responsible (*metaitios*) for these things; you singly have done everything – you are all-responsible (*panaitios*)'. Orestes, however, claims that Apollo shares in responsibility (*metaitios*), and Apollo, although he says he himself will be Orestes' advocate and takes on himself the responsibility for the matricide, does share in the process of the trial. The attribution of responsibility is again part of the *agon* of accusation and counter-accusation, here involving Apollo, the Furies and

Orestes – an Olympian god, chthonic deities and a mortal. The trial – an institution set up to determine responsibility and blame – indicates in its shared advocacy a shared responsibility between god and man, and a complex dialectic between gods. In the network of causes and consequences that surrounds each event of the *Oresteia*, divine necessity plays a part that is far from 'simple and practical'.

The complexity of the representation of human and divine interaction is also in part due to the complex representation of the figures of the gods themselves. Zeus – as always in Greek tragedy – appears only in the words of others, but the Furies and Apollo in particular are mentioned throughout the first two plays of the trilogy, before their appearance in the *Eumenides*. Nor is it easy to arrive at a single composite picture or evaluation of the representation (Brown). The Furies appear first as agents of the justice of Zeus in the opening choral ode of the *Agamemnon*. So too the arrival of Helen at Troy – 'a spirit of windless calm' (*Aga.* 740) – turns out to be the arrival of a Fury sent by Zeus (*Aga.* 749) – as if the arrival of Helen was itself the embodiment of a Fury, rather than the transgression to be punished by a Fury. The house of Agamemnon is said by Cassandra, as we have seen, to be inhabited by (*Aga.* 1187–90) 'a band of celebrating Furies who have drunk on human blood' – where the Furies stand for and enact the intrafamilial violence and revenge. At the end of the *Choephoroi*, it is 'like Gorgons, hair woven with snakes, black-robed' (*Cho.* 1048–9) that the Furies appear to Orestes. This is a sign of his madness, a vision, the chorus claims. Yet these 'hounds of the mother' make up the chorus of the *Eumenides* (seen by all) where they speak both as representatives of Clytemnestra pursuing vengeance for a mother's blood and, more generally, as figures who maintain the justice or order of things. At the end of the play, they are less specifically tied to blood vengeance and more generally figured as maintainers of order within household and *polis*, as they take up their position on the Acropolis, where in Aeschylus' fifth-century Athens they were indeed worshipped as the Revered Ones (*Semnai*). There is, then, a certain fluctuation as the Furies appear both as the agents of Zeus and as opposed to Apollo, the agent of Zeus; as sign of madness and maintainers of justice; as blood-curdling instantiations of revenge for crimes of blood, and the preservers of social order.

Apollo, the Olympian god, has proved as difficult for critics to evaluate. Although he appears as the inspirer of Cassandra and the motivator of Orestes, it is primarily his role in the trial that has polarized reactions to this divine figure. For some critics, Apollo is the god of truth and purity, whose support of Orestes leads to a triumph of civilized values over the blood-lust of revenge. For others, his notorious argument that the mother cannot truly be called parent and his abuse of the Furies when crossed, have led to characterizations of Apollo as a 'shyster lawyer', and his performance has been called an attempt to discredit the oracle of Delphi for its support of Persia in the recent wars. What is crucial to both of these overexaggerated portraits is that Apollo, who declares that he speaks the truth, does not win over the human jury – the votes remain tied. Similarly Athene, much as her remarks on the role of men and women echo some of Apollo's argument, also closely recalls some of the Furies' remarks about fear and justice – before voting against them. There is, in other words, agreement neither between the divine figures of the play nor in the human reactions to the divine figures. The clashing of competing obligations that has characterized the human action in the tragedy is mirrored on the divine level – which reminds us just how difficult it is for a modern Western audience to come to terms with the literature, belief and practice of a polytheistic system.

The divine frame is crucial to a sense of human place and order. Yet the framing does not provide an easy control or simple determination of human events. Aeschylus depicts the relations between men and gods as a shifting source of fear, doubt and loss as well as celebration, support and order.

If in the first part of this chapter – 'A charter for the city?' – we saw how the *Oresteia* moved towards at least a conditional celebration of the order of the *polis*, in this second part we have seen how Aeschylus' consideration of man's place within the systems of order also represents ignorance, uncertainty and lack of control as basic to humans' lives. This tension between the doubts and fears of human existence and the glories of the *polis* (the frame for that existence) remains central to the tragic narrative of Aeschylus, and to the complex portrayal of human action in the *Oresteia*.

The poetic texture

I have already quoted in translation several key passages of the *Oresteia* and tried where possible to indicate some of the difficulties and ambiguities of translation. It would be hard to write with any care about Aeschylus without facing such problems, since the poetry with which every scene and every chorus is composed is remarkably dense and remarkably complex in its cumulative effects. Almost any passage could be chosen to highlight the texture of what is some of the most extraordinary dramatic poetry ever written – perhaps only some of late Shakespeare comes close – but I have chosen three short passages, one from each play, which both draw together some of the themes of the previous discussions and indicate some of the range of this writing. For each, I have chosen an influential and well-known English translation (or translations) so that we may also view the variety of response of translators and explore the types of choices with which they are faced.

13 The intensity of lyric prophecy

The first passage I have chosen is from the first choral ode of the *Agamemnon*, and it is the last two lines of Calchas' prophecy. It is lyric poetry, to be sung with musical accompaniment by the chorus, and I will offer first a transcription:

> *mimnei gar phobera palinortos*
> *oikonomos dolia mnamōn mēnis teknopoinos.*

Lloyd-Jones translates as follows:

> For there abides, terrible, ever again arising,
> a keeper of the house guileful, unforgetting, Wrath child-avenging.

Fagles, however, translates:

> Here she waits
> the terror raging back and back in the future
>   the stealth, the law of the hearth, the mother –
>   Memory womb of Fury child-avenging Fury!

The situation will be recalled: the omen of the eagles has led Calchas to worry that another terrible sacrifice will be required.

These lines express the reason why he has such a fear. It is a passage central to the idea of the household's curse, to the narrative of revenge and to the themes of terror, intrafamilial violence and the effects of the past on the present. Its complexity – that allows two such different translations! – stems from its syntax, its vocabulary and the way its imagery is linked into the whole narrative of the trilogy. Let me gloss the passage: *mimnei gar*, 'for there remains': emphatically placed first word, the verb 'there remains' indicates a constancy within the pattern of events that have already been described. This verb will also be used, for example, for the inevitable pattern of reversal and revenge that is Zeus's law (*Aga.* 1563–4): **mimnei** *de* **mimnontos** *en thronōi Dios, pathein ton erxanta*, 'It remains a sign of Zeus who *remains* on his throne, that the doer suffers.' So, it occurs throughout the trilogy as characters search for stability amid the shifting determination of events. Here, then, the reason offered why another sacrifice might be required is because of what remains constant.

The subject of this verb is all the remaining words of the passage. What remains is, first, *phobera*, 'fearsome'. We have seen how terror is a pervasive mood haunting the *Oresteia*. Here, what remains is immediately frightening – this passage looks forward to all those future fears for which the omen and the curse play such a part. What remains is also *palinortos*. Unlike the first three words of the line, this is an extremely uncommon poetic adjective (that, in fact, occurs only here in surviving Greek texts). It suggests 'rising up back again'. *Palin*, the first part of what is a compound adjective, implies precisely the logic of reversal and repetition ('back again') central to revenge; and the verb stem from which *-ortos* comes suggests 'rising', 'rushing', 'incited' – that is, what remains is also active and activated, hence Fagles' 'back and back in the future', a bold attempt to capture the force of the adjective.

What remains is also *oikonomos*. Here is the first noun of the sentence. *Oikonomos* means 'household manager' (the term from which 'economics' is derived). The noun directs attention to the *oikos* as the focus of the narrative. Although Agamemnon is with the army, the sacrifice is caused by something that directs the household. It is this term, primarily, that provides the sense of a specifically familial horror. It is also a surprising term that suggests both the household manager Clytemnestra (whom we have heard of ordering – managing – the watchman) and the idea of a more general force directing the household members (the overlap suggests how Clytemnestra fulfils a role in the family history and how the family history finds an instrument in Clytemnestra).

The other noun in the sentence, however, is *mēnis*, 'wrath', 'violent anger'. This is the first word of the *Iliad* and one of its key themes – the violent, destructive anger of the hero Achilles. In that work, it is used only of Achilles and the gods and stresses a particular force of rage. With these two nouns, however, we must note the difficulty of the syntax, and in two ways. First, it is quite unclear which of the two nouns is subject of the sentence, which in apposition. That is, does it mean 'violent anger remains, a fearful rising back up again household manager'; or does it mean 'the fearful rising back up again household manager remains, violent anger'? Secondly, it is unclear which noun is qualified by the two adjectives, *dolia* and *mnamōn*, that come between the two nouns (or whether *dolia* is even a noun, 'a deceptive woman'). Most editors take *dolia* with *oikonomos* and *mnamōn* with *mēnis*, 'deceptive household manager', 'remembering wrath', but it remains strictly uncertain, and possibly both adjectives can qualify both nouns. Fagles attempts to maintain the ambiguity by translating *dolia* as 'the stealth' and leaving it juxtaposed to the other words of the sentence; Lloyd-Jones by closely following the word order of the Greek. *Dolia* means 'deceptive' and when taken closely with *oikonomos* suggests both the specific deception of Clytemnestra, and the way in which the narrative of revenge in the house will repeatedly depend on deception. It is precisely *dolia peithō*, 'deceptive persuasion' that the chorus prays to help Orestes as he enters the palace. *Oikonomos dolia*, 'deceptive household manager', may also recall, however, by contrast Penelope, Odysseus' wife, who maintains her house by deception in the *Odyssey*. (We have seen the inevitable association between the two households in Greek literature since the *Odyssey*.) As much as Orestes is a model for Telemachus in the *Odyssey*, so Penelope and Clytemnestra are explicitly contrasted more than once in the epic. *Oikonomos dolia*, 'deceptive household manager', points thus to the different evaluations of deceptive women within the exemplary text of the patriarchal *oikos*. If *dolia* is taken closely with *mēnis*, 'deceptive wrath', however, it indicates the way in which the violent anger which motivates revenge hides itself and uses deception to achieve its end.

Mnamōn denotes 'remembering' and strengthens the sense of *mimnei*, 'remains'. What remains does not pass into obscurity or neglect over time (but 'rises back up again'). If it is taken closely with *oikonomos*, it implies both the way that Clytemnestra has nurtured her hatred over the years, and the way in which Agamemnon's ten-year absence from the house will not prevent the curse of the house recalling his transgression and demanding payment. If it is taken closely with *mēnis*, it implies that the 'violent anger' does not pass into reconciliation (as, say, at the end of the *Iliad*) but harbours its rage.

The final adjective is *teknopoinos* and, like so many compound adjectives in Greek, it can have an active and a passive sense, both 'avenging a child' and 'avenged by a child'. What I have translated as 'avenging'/'avenged', namely *poin-*, is a term that repeatedly occurs in the trilogy and connotes both punishment and payment – central to the social language of exchange and justice. The word 'child', *teknon*, it need hardly be emphasized, is one of the commonest terms in the trilogy: we have already seen how it becomes invested with special force not merely in the discussions of the trial scene, but also in the language of childbirth and of parental characteristics that is used to express the connection between events in precisely the narrative of punishment and payment (*poin-*). The ambiguity between active and passive readings of the adjective is highly significant. For the history of revenge is also a history of violence between the generations, where parents and children repeatedly act against each other and to avenge each other. Agamemnon kills his daughter, and Clytemnestra takes revenge for her death. Orestes kills his mother, a child avenging a parent, and even Aegisthus sees his role in the death of Agamemnon as repaying on the child of Atreus the sins of Atreus against the children of Thyestes, Aegisthus' father. The final adjective of this line encapsulates in its ambiguity the narrative of inter-generational violence, and the narrative of repeated punishment.

The first two words of Calchas' prophetic statement, then, promise an explanation (*gar*, 'for') and state that something remains. As the sentence progresses, however, both the involved syntax and the layered implications of the vocabulary transform the explanation into an obscure and darkening impression of the motive force directing this narrative. The combination of the lyric compactness and prophetic allusiveness produces an expression that connects a set of terms in a network of interrelations that continue to find further significance throughout the *Oresteia*. Such intricate and intense poetry is typical of Aeschylean choral lyric, particularly in the *Oresteia*: the linguistic texture weaves together with a conceptual patterning to produce a powerful all-embracing expression of things, a cosmology.

14 Violent exchange: dramatic dialogue

The second passage I wish to consider is taken from the *Choephoroi* and it is a passage from the highly dramatic dialogue as Clytemnestra and Orestes come face to face. Again I will first transliterate the Greek and then offer a translation, this time from Grene and Lattimore (though without their stage-directions):

Clyt.	*ti esti khrēma? tina boēn histēs domois?*
Servant	*ton zōnta kainein tous tethnēkotas legō.*
Clyt.	*oi' gō, xunēka toupos ex ainigmatōn.*
	dolois oloumeth' hōsper oun ekteinamen.
	doiē tis androkmēta pelekun hōs takhos.
	eidōmen ei nikōmen ē nikōmetha.
	entautha gar dē toud' aphikomēn kakou.
Orestes	*se kai mateuō. tōide d'arkountōs ekhei.*
Clyt.	*oi' gō, tethnēkas, philtat' Aigisthou bia.*
Orestes	*phileis ton andra? toigar en tautōi taphōi*
	keisēi, thanonta d' outi mē prodōis pote.

Clyt.	What is this and why are you shouting in the house?
Servant	I tell you, he is alive and killing the dead.
Clyt.	Ah so. You speak in riddles but I read the rhyme.
	We have been won with treachery by which we slew.
	Bring me quick, somebody, an axe to kill a man,
	And we shall see if we can beat him before we
	go down – so far gone are we in this wretched fight.
Orestes	You next: the other one in there has had enough.
Clyt.	Beloved, strong Aegisthus, are you dead indeed?
Orestes	You love your man? You shall lie in the same grave
	With him, and never be unfaithful even in death.

Clytemnestra asks what the noise in the house is and the servant replies with a riddling utterance which not only avoids the names of Aegisthus and Orestes, but also syntactically could be translated either 'the dead are killing the living' or 'the living are killing the dead' – an ambiguity inevitably lost in English. (In each case, 'the dead', *tous tethnēkotas*, is a plural term, 'the living', *ton zōnta*, singular.) The first interpretation is that which is to be privileged; it implies both that Orestes, believed dead, is killing Aegisthus; and, further, that Agamemnon, whose help from the tomb was invoked and conjured in the *kommos*, is being avenged; and even that the whole history of death in the house is claiming another victim. Clytemnestra solves the riddle and perceives immediately the logic of revenge and reversal: *dolois oloumeth' hōsper oun ekteinamen*, 'we are being destroyed by deception [*dolois*] as we killed', or as Grene and Lattimore put it, 'we have been won with treachery by which we slew'. As we have seen, communication is a central theme of the *Oresteia*, and as Clytemnestra's verbal dexterity led Agamemnon to his doom, and as a verbal trick has allowed Orestes safe access to the palace, and a changed message has tricked Aegisthus to return unguarded to his death, so a riddle – a deceptive utterance that reveals the truth – is the means by which Clytemnestra learns of her impending fate. Throughout the *Oresteia*, there are riddles and solutions, riddles that remain riddles – all these are scenes of sign-reading. This dialogue, apparently unnecessarily framed as a riddle and solution, directs attention to a link in the narrative chain, a thematic continuity.

The destruction by deception, *dolois*, not only recalls the deceptive (*dolia*) element of the curse I discussed in the previous passage, but also specifically Orestes' own description of Apollo's command (*Cho.* 556–7), where he says 'as they killed an honoured man by deception [*dolōi*], so they are to be taken by a deception [*dolōi*]'. Clytemnestra's words unwittingly also fulfil the terms of Apollo's oracle. Human language is more telling than the speaker can know.

Clytemnestra calls for someone to bring her as quickly as possible an *androkmēta pelekun*, 'an axe to kill a man', as Grene and Lattimore translate. The adjective *androkmēta*, 'man-killing', 'man-wearying', points towards the gender struggle in two ways. First, it recalls her killing of her 'man', her husband (*andro-* means both 'man' and 'husband'); secondly, the axe is to be a defence against Orestes, who is trying to achieve the status of 'man' – the full status of adult male in charge of his own house. She expresses this conflict with her son as 'Let us see if we have the victory [*nikōmen*] or the victory is over us [*nikōmetha*]' (the repetition of the same verb is unfortunately lost in Grene and Lattimore's version). This idea of *nikē*, 'victory', is extremely important in the *Oresteia*, primarily for the way it is repeatedly used to express the sense of struggle for dominance in conflict. 'Victory' is the aim of each *agon* – until Athene and the Furies, where Athene says (*Eum.* 795), 'For you have not given up the victory, *ou gar nenikesth.*' Here, Clytemnestra captures perfectly the sense of mutually exclusive possibilities of the polarized gender conflict: either absolute victory or absolute defeat. *Nikē*, 'victory', however, also constantly resonates with that other key term of the narrative of conflict, *dikē*. So, Athene continues to the Furies after the trial's vote 'For you have not given up the victory . . . *all' isopsēphos dikē*', 'but the *dikē* has been of equal votes'. As Orestes arrives as the agent of *dikē*, the sense of *dikē* as revenge, destruction or punishment is significantly qualified by the description of the conflict as the pursuit of *nikē*.

Orestes enters: *se kai mateuō*, 'You I track too.' Grene and Lattimore leave out the verb, but *mateuō*, 'I track', is properly used of dogs on the scent, and thus Orestes represents himself as hunter (as he will become the hunted victim of the 'dogs of his mother'). The 'tricky hunter' (*dolois . . . mateuō*) is a figure often associated in Greek culture with the hunt of the young male as he is being initiated into the world of the adult men (Vidal-Naquet). As Orestes approaches the killing of his mother, he is also depicted as approaching the status of manhood. The man-killing axe may prevent him reaching manhood.

Clytemnestra recognizes from Orestes' dismissive comment (*tōide d'arkountōs ekhei*, 'he's had enough' – a dismissal typical of the lack of concern with which Aegisthus' death is treated in Aeschylus as opposed to in Homer) that her 'most beloved', *philtat'*, is dead. Orestes picks up both her terms *philtat'* and *androkmēta*, 'man-wearying', as he asks *phileis ton andra*, 'You love this man?' Yet it is misleading to translate the verb *phileis* simply as 'you love', as it so often is. For the term implies in Greek a sense of mutual obligation and duty more than an affective or romantic tie. Orestes, by using the term, is emphasizing his reaction to her adultery as a social transgression – a crime against her husband (*andra*) and a failure of her obligations and duty to the household. So, he concludes with fine rhetoric, 'Then you will lie in the same tomb. Never again betray the dead man [*thanonta*].' Grene and Lattimore's translation 'never be un-faithful even in death' (apart from adding the emphasis of 'even') misses the point of *thanonta*, 'the dead man', because it refers at one level to Aegisthus with whom she will ever lie in death – faithful to her adultery; but on another level it refers to Agamemnon, the other dead man, whom she will never again betray (with Aegisthus). Orestes' remark recalls the servant's riddle of 'the dead are killing the living', as Clytemnestra is killed for killing her man. Orestes' comment, then, stresses the adultery as much as the murder as the reason for her punishment.

This is a piece of highly charged dramatic dialogue that is both fast and forceful. It is also an intricately layered exchange which situates the stage action of the confrontation of mother and son within a network of thematic structures. I have described at length the way in which Aeschylus develops a highly involved view of human action: here we can see how the language of dialogue at a moment of crucial dramatic action works to develop this sense of the complex nature of events.

15 Political rhetoric

For my final passage I wish to look at some lines from the *Eumenides* where Athene establishes the court of the Areopagus. It is in such writing that Aeschylus' direct involvement with the *polis*, his audience, has been most repeatedly discussed; it will also offer an opportunity, after a lyric ode and a piece of dialogue, to consider a lengthy set speech (*rhēsis*), another basic part of Aeschylean dra-maturgy. I can, however, consider only a few lines from the speech here. Athene has described the setting of the Areopagus as the hill (*pagos*) where Theseus, king of Athens, sacrificed to the god of war (*Ares*) before his battle with the Amazons. The establishment of the court is thus immediately linked into the corpus of the city's myths. Theseus is a founding figure of the *polis* of Athens as a *polis*. The Amazons (depicted on so many temples and other art works) are archetypally negative female figures who reverse all the expectations of a female's role, not least in their violent, armed hostility to men: this may, then, be thought to be significantly invoked before the trial of Clytemnestra. Athene continues (*Eum.* 690–9):

> en de tōi sebas
> astōn phobos te xungenēs to mē adikein
> skhēsei to t' ēmar kai kat' euphronēn homōs,
> autōn politōn mē 'pikainontōn nomous;
> kakais epirroaisi borborōi th' hudōr
> lampron miainōn oupoth' heurēseis poton.
> to mēt' anarkhon mēte despotoumenon
> astois peristellousi bouleuō sebein
> kai mē to deinon pan poleōs exōbalein.

Tony Harrison's version of the *Oresteia*, produced first at the National Theatre, London, has this:

> The people's reverence and the fear they're born with
> will restrain them day and night from acts of injustice
> as long as they don't foul their own laws with defilement.
> No one should piss in the well they draw drink from.
> Anarchy! Tyranny! Let both be avoided
> nor banish fear from your city entirely.

Every word of this passage is charged with significance both from the narrative of the play and from its political context in the theatre. *Sebas*, translated 'reverence', indicates the 'respect' which allows hierarchical order to be maintained. It is precisely lack of *sebas* in the *Choephoroi* that characterized the disorder in the house of Agamemnon. Now the term spreads from the household to the political sphere of the Athenian 'people' – *astōn*, the general term which includes free-born men and women. There may be a fascinating ambiguity, however, in the phrase *sebas astōn*. For does it imply 'the respect of citizens' for the Areopagus – that is, law-abidingness depends on the citizens' respect for the institutions of law? Or does it imply the respect *for* the citizens that the Areopagus is to show – that is, an executive judicial body in a democracy is accountable to the people, and the law-court itself must respect the citizens? Either reading is semantically and grammatically possible – and the ambiguity significantly traces the range of political opinions present in the turmoil of the reforms of the Areopagus. Who is to be accountable to whom?

Along with respect comes *phobos*, 'fear': the term which has pervaded the *Oresteia* now becomes a positive emotion in the prevention of injustice. This fear is *xungenēs*, which may imply 'kindred', that is 'of the same race', as the 'respect'; or it may mean 'in-born', that 'they're born with' – the inherited characteristic of the race which has been a thematic focus of the narrative, as we have seen. Now it is a propensity to avoid wrong-doing (*adikein*, the negative of *dikē*) that is passed on with the new institution of law. This 'respect and fear' will prevent crime 'day and night'. This is not just an expression for 'always', but also recalls the imagery of light and darkness that is so common in the *Oresteia*, imagery which has developed an association of crime with darkness, obscurity, hidden deceptions. (So, too, the Furies are daughters of Night.) Seen or unseen, this restraint of wrong-doing will operate. Yet its operation depends on the citizens (*politōn*, the full term for 'citizens') not innovating or fouling their laws. (The Greek verb is unfortunately meaningless through manuscript corruption: 'innovate' translates the commonest emendation; Harrison's 'foul' a less common suggestion.) This political message is supported by an appeal to the world of nature: clean water for drinking is not to be polluted with 'evil influxes' – 'piss', as Harrison characteristically puts it. The 'natural' values of purity and cleanliness as opposed to evil and pollution bolster the goddess' institution.

Yet what is the political message? Some critics have claimed that Athene speaks quite generally: a well-organized society is distinguished by the stability of its legal system. In particular, the Athenian law on homicide could not – by law – be changed (Macleod). Yet since this is a speech on the Areopagus and the political debates over the Areopagus had been so violent in Athens, most critics have seen Athene's remarks as more pointed. Yet here too debate has been heated. Some critics have seen Aeschylus as speaking out against the reform of the Areopagus, since the court receives in Athene's speech such praise, and so strong is the injunction not to innovate: the court is, she says, established for all time. Other critics, however, have pointed out that Ephialtes' reforms made changes to the Areopagus on the ground that 'accretions' had to be removed:

the Areopagus should be returned to its original and proper function. Thus, it is argued, when Athene warns the citizens, here at the first trial by the Areopagus, not to make innovations in the laws of her institution, the goddess of the city is to be seen as supporting Ephialtes' democratic programme (Dover). Other critics yet think that while the Ephialtic reforms are accepted, this speech warns against any further change, since further reforms were in the air in 458 B.C.

Now, much of Athene's speech addresses the ideals of the democratic *polis*. So the belief in 'respect', 'justice', 'the laws' leads in the remaining lines to a ringing denunciation of both anarchy and tyranny (words which closely echo the Furies' own advice on justice, who had sung (525–6) 'Praise neither the anarchic life nor life under a tyrant', *mēt'anarkton bion mēte despotoumenon ainesēis*). This polarization of lawlessness and tyranny constructs democracy as the necessary and proper middle ground. This is the counsel (*bouleuō*) of Athene, her official advice, that neither 'respect' (*sebein*, recalling *sebas*) nor 'the awesome' (*to deinon*, parallel to *phobos*, 'fear') – both terms are rendered as 'fear' by Harrison – should be cast from the *polis*, the frame of the speech. The explicit remark about innovation and the law, then, is surrounded by a repeated appeal to respect and dread as political virtues – the most general and non-partisan of evaluative terms (Dodds; Meier). Any specific point is thus framed by a general concern for the well-being of the city.

Athene's emphasis here and elsewhere on national well-being and the avoidance of civic discord and wrong-doing makes it hard to discover a single 'partisan' political viewpoint with any security; so too the specific remarks on innovation, as we have seen, are open to different readings. Perhaps it is best, then, to conclude with Sommerstein that 'each spectator will understand it in the light of his own preconceptions'. Or, as with the other aspects of Aeschylean poetry and drama that I have been discussing in this book, the political discourse of the *Oresteia* maps out a site of engagement, not a scene of straight-forward didacticism.

Chapter 3

The influence of the *Oresteia*

16 *From Sophocles to the women's movement*

A detailed portrait of some two thousand years of literary and dramatic influence of this Landmark is out of the question here. Rather than let this final chapter lapse into little more than a series of names or list of famous performances, I have chosen three key moments from the intellectual and literary after-life of this great work.

The first and most obvious area of influence is on the other great Athenian dramatists, Euripides and Sophocles. Both returned constantly to the *Oresteia*. There are innumerable echoes of language, dramatic technique and staging throughout their surviving works, but it is in particular in each playwright's *Electra* that the anxiety of influence is most strongly in evidence. Unfortunately, the relative dates of Euripides' and Sophocles' plays are unknown. But both take as their model the *Oresteia*, and in particular the *Choephoroi*. I shall look briefly therefore at each of these plays' rewriting of Aeschylus' rewriting of Homer.

The corpus of Sophocles' work is dominated by the pathology of extremism. In each play, he represents figures who are fiercely committed to personal honour, personal success, who come into increasingly bitter and unrelenting conflict with society, and who usually end at violent odds with the collective. This so-called Sophoclean hero (Knox; Winnington-Ingram; Segal) enacts the paradox that to achieve greatness is to go beyond the bounds of acceptability: transgression and outstandingness both involve going too far. Yet in his *Electra*, the focus is not on Orestes – Aeschylus' paradigm – but firmly on Electra. (Sophocles' play is a single drama: the other plays of his trilogy for the competition were on unrelated subjects – although they may, of course, have been thematically connected.) It is Electra's passionate and violent commitment to revenge with its emotional and ethical distortions that is centre stage. Indeed, Orestes enters in the first scene with Pylades, exits when he hears Electra's first cry from inside the house, and is not seen again until the last scene of the play, the revenge itself. It is this final scene – full of verbal echoes of Aeschylus – that shows most clearly how Sophocles' *Electra* works against the *Oresteia*. Orestes confronts and kills his mother inside the house, while Electra is alone on stage with the chorus. In a thrillingly horrific scene, we hear from inside the house Clytemnestra echoing Aeschylus' Clytemnestra as she begs her son for mercy. Yet we do not hear any response from Orestes. Instead, Electra screams 'hit her again, hit her again'. Where in Aeschylus' play the mother's appeal led to a famous moment of hesitation and ratification with Pylades' authorization of the killing according to the gods' oracle, here we do not see either hesitation or ratification. Rather, what is dramatized is Electra's passionate commitment to the killing. No doubts.

Indeed, after Clytemnestra has been killed, Orestes leads Aegisthus back into the house, and there the plays ends. No madness and pursuit by the Furies. No Athens and no law-court; no discussion and voting on the action. The final word of the play is 'ended' (*tel-*) – and there could be few more striking comparisons with Aeschylus: the *Oresteia* with its torch-lit procession of the city; the *Electra* with its exit into the silent, dark and murderous house. This silence about the matricide is followed through the play. There is almost no discussion of its validity, and there are only two brief and ambiguous mentions of the oracle, and scarcely more direct concern with the divine motivation so important to the *Oresteia*. For some readers, therefore, Sophocles' play has been seen as a turning away from Aeschylean problematics back to Homer, where Orestes was the exemplary hero. For others, the play dramatizes the god-ordered necessity of requital, grim but inevitable. For others still, the tragedy is precisely Orestes' failure to ask the right questions – a moral obtuseness that leads to the violent horror of matricide. One thing at least is clear. Sophocles has taken away from his play all the apparatus of judgement and evaluation that dominates Aeschylus' writing – all the discussions and redefinitions of events leading to the formal judgement of the trial. Sophocles makes the audience the trial and jury of events, turns on the audience the problem of evaluating the represented matricide. Sophocles' silence enjoins the audience's engagement.

If Sophocles' Orestes kills without the play passing judgement, in Euripides' *Electra* there is the most direct and negative evaluation of Orestes. The god Castor, who appears in the final scene to bring the play to a close, says Clytemnestra may have received *dikē*, but 'you did not do *dikē*'. Orestes in Homer was exemplary; in Aeschylus, an example of the tragic double bind; in Sophocles, unjudged, but also unpraised; in Euripides, he is said by the god simply to have done wrong in killing his mother.

Yet the most obvious echo of Aeschylus occurs in the recognition scene of the play. Electra – in a typically Euripidean twist – has been married to a poor farmer (although her marriage has not been consummated). Orestes, after visiting the tomb of their father, has come in disguise to visit the outlying farm. An old man comes via the tomb and declares to Electra that her brother has returned home. He offers three proofs of Orestes' return, and they are precisely the three tokens Aeschylus had used in that most difficult scene of the *Choephoroi* – the lock of hair, the footprint and a piece of cloth. Electra in Euripides, far from leaping into the recognition of her beloved brother, dismisses each token with fine rationalism: a man's hair and a woman's are not the same, and anyway people of the same family often have dissimilar hair; the ground is too rocky for footprints; and, unless Orestes' clothes grow with his legs, he cannot be wearing a piece of cloth she had made – had she even been old enough to weave when Orestes left. This scene has often outraged sober scholars with its evident parody of Aeschylus. There is a serious point, however, as Electra's rationalism leads to the wrong conclusion – one more error of judgement in this play's anatomy of how false evaluations, particularly misleading commitments to heroic paradigms, collectively lead to the violence of tragedy.

Both Euripides and Sophocles explicitly and at length work with and against their great predecessor. From this interplay of writers comes the inheritance of Western drama.

The second moment I wish to mention is the flourishing of the study of Greece in German Romantic culture of the nineteenth century in particular. This has been called quite fairly the tyranny of Greece over the German imagination – and it is a tyranny that stretches from Winckelmann and Hegel on to Marx and Freud. Classical Greek culture was the privileged object of study throughout the German education system of the period, and to understand the intellectual life of the era it is necessary to appreciate the engagement with Greek literature. It is easy to find worship of Aeschylus: Schlegel, for example, wrote of Aeschylus 'in his almost superhuman greatness he is likely to remain unexcelled'. Yet perhaps the most influential joint readers of Aeschylus were Nietzsche and Wagner. For Wagner, Greek drama was 'the highest conceivable form of art', a view he discussed at length with Nietzsche, while Nietzsche was producing *The Birth of Tragedy from the Spirit of Music*, a work in which Aeschylus constitutes the pinnacle of ancient and thus all art (Silk and Stern). In his autobiography, Wagner recalls movingly his first readings of Aeschylus 'with real feeling and understanding': 'I could see the *Oresteia* with my mind's eye, as though it were actually being performed and its effect on me was undescribable. Nothing could equal the sublime emotion with which the *Agamemnon* inspired me; and to the last word of the *Eumenides*, I remained in an atmosphere so far removed from the present day that I have never since been really able to reconcile myself with modern literature. My ideas about the whole significance of drama and the theatre were no doubt moulded by these impressions.' So the *Ring* in its final form has four plays – three tragedies and a lighter piece, though for Wagner the lighter piece comes before the tragedies, whereas the satyr play came after the tragedies in ancient Athens. The *Ring* is made up of a thematically linked cycle of mythic stories; it is focused on a curse, which connects events and produces an oppressive and memory-laden narrative; the story is of conflictual relations between men, gods, monsters, and between the genders; there is a political thrust to the reworking of inherited myths. These are all striking elements of the *Ring* that Wagner expressly develops from Aeschylus and the *Oresteia*. Even Wagner's famous leitmotif technique of composition by repeated musical mottoes owes something to Aeschylus' systems of repeated images.

Wagner hoped especially to recreate what he called the *Gesamtkunstwerk*, the 'combined' or 'total' work of art, which he saw embodied in Greek tragedy, but lost to Western culture since – an art work which combined music, theatre, myth, intellect, politics, dance. In this spirit, Wagner required his operas to be performed as part of a special festival, Bayreuth, where, he intended, art could be for the whole populace, not merely the patron and the industrialist; where the social and intellectual context of Greek drama could be recreated – that awesome spectacle the Athenians attended 'to see the image of themselves, to read the riddle of their action, to fuse their own being and their communion with that of their god'.

Wagner's representation and re-creation of ancient Greece owe a lot to an idealization common to much nineteenth-century writing. Yet Wagner looked for no slavish imitation: he engaged with Aeschylus, tested his own ideas against his model of Greece, but still saw his own work as revolutionary (like Aeschylus' own reworkings of Homer). The final image of *Götterdämmerung* makes this point in strikingly dramatic fashion, as indeed it draws its significance from the *Oresteia*. For Wagner's work ends with torches, but a procession to the violent destruction of the home of the gods – as the 'gods have had to surrender their direct influence, faced with the freedom of human consciousness'. It is this late Romantic sentiment of Wagner's 'twilight of the gods', so alien to Greek writing, that, no less than Nietzsche's 'death of god', heralds the modern era.

My third moment relates more specifically to the theme of gender in the *Oresteia*. In the 1830s, J. J. Bachofen, a Swiss jurist, wrote an influential book called *Das Mutterrecht*, 'Mother-right', in which he outlined a universal pattern of social development away from an original matriarchy to the present patriarchal order. Much of his evidence was classical – inevitably for nineteenth-century Europe – and the *Oresteia* with its devaluation of the cause of the female and its support of the cause of the male in the trial scene became a key piece of evidence for the overthrow of women's original rights. (I have already mentioned how modern anthropological readings of 'the myth of matriarchy overthrown' differ from this approach: no historical matriarchy, it is generally accepted, has ever existed.) His views, however, were fundamental to Engels' central thesis on the development of the family, private property and the state, and Freud too echoes them when he sees the *Oresteia* as 'an echo of this revolution . . . this turning from the mother to the father [which] signifies a victory of spirituality over the senses – that is to say, a step forward in culture'. With the rise of the women's movement this century, Bachofen and his reading of the *Oresteia* returned to the fore of discussion. Kate Millett, for example, in *Sexual Politics* attacks Athene for her support of the male: 'She marches on spoiling to destroy her kind . . . this sort of corroboration can be fatal'; and she dismisses the final scenes of the *Oresteia* as 'five pages of local chamber of commerce rhapsody' that charts 'this triumph of patriarchy'. Although such a reading of the *Oresteia* as a historical document that simply records or even echoes the overthrow of a historical matriarchy is not adopted by many scholars these days, none the less such discussions have kept the *Oresteia* on the agenda. One of the most influential pieces of modern feminist writing is Hélène Cixous' marvellous 'Sorties'. This extended essay weaves together fragments of Cixous' biography with readings of classical and modern texts, as it explores the representation of femininity in Western culture. It shows something of Aeschylus' intense lyricism and polemicism as it uses its language to disrupt what it sees as the order and control of patriarchy. It is in this, as much as in its readings themselves, that Cixous' essay has become emblematic for a series of feminist writers. Under the heading 'The Dawn of Phallocentrism', Freud, Joyce, Kafka lead to a reflection on how the language of the Electra plays – she regularly conflates Aeschylus, Euripides and Sophocles – combines with the discussion of language-use in the plays and the performance of language – its shrieks, silences, insinuations – to produce both the 'bloody dawn of phallocentrism' in the murder of the mother and the continual unquenchable voice of Electra's pain: 'Who stays behind? In the end, only sister Electra orests . . . A stream of cries that won't run out, torment's spring that won't run dry: she has to yell, vomit – torrential – this flood that results from paternal torture is bottomless, all the spilled blood, all the lost sperm run, inexhaustible, through this strange gorge, through which from the most distant burial, the father returns. The father, strongest of all, carries off the tongue that calls and projects him. "Viper's tongue!" says Clytemnestra.'

These all too brief discussions indicate some points at which the engagement with Aeschylus has been particularly productive, particularly fascinating. My hope is that this book will enable other, new readers to start on what may be a lengthy but rich encounter.

Guide to further reading

Sections 1, 2, 3 of this guide contain the works mentioned in the text, listed in alphabetical order. Works marked with an asterisk require a knowledge of Greek. The opening section contains the standard editions and translations and some general works on Aeschylus and Greek tragedy with comments.

Editions

Agamemnon: *E. Fraenkel (Oxford, 1950); *J. D. Denniston and D. L. Page (Oxford, 1957). Both are very scholarly on the language, but less useful on literary or theatrical interpretation. *Choephoroi:* *A. Garvie (Oxford, 1986); very useful for the scholar, and with helpful indications of further reading. *Eumenides:* *A. Sommerstein (Cambridge, 1991), a fine edition; A. Podlecki (Warminster, 1987); rather plodding, but for the non-Greek reader.

Translations

Good basic translations are: C. Collard, *Aeschylus Oresteia* (Oxford, 2002); R. Fagles, *Aeschylus: the Oresteia* (New York, 1966); D. Grene and R. Lattimore, *Complete Greek Tragedies*, vol. 1 (Chicago, 1959); H. Lloyd-Jones, *Aeschylus: Oresteia* (London, 1982); P. Vellacott, *The Oresteia* (Harmondsworth, 1974). Poetic versions, rather than simple translations: Tony Harrison, *The Oresteia* (London, 1981); Ted Hughes, *The Oresteia by Aeschylus* (New York, 1998).

There is no general book on the *Oresteia* that is recommendable for the reader who does not know Greek. My *Reading Greek Tragedy* (Cambridge, 1986) is an advanced critical introduction to Greek tragedy with two chapters on the *Oresteia*. D. Conacher, *Aeschylus' Oresteia: a Literary Commentary* (Toronto, 1987) is a very traditional scene by scene reading, which misses much of the complexity of the trilogy. J. Herington's *Aeschylus* (Yale, 1986) has a useful introduction to the fragments, but is rather waffly otherwise. On the politics of Aeschylean theatre, see the lively debate between M. Griffith, 'Brilliant Dynasts: Power and Politics in the *Oresteia*', *Classical Antiquity*, vol. 15, 1995; J. Griffin, 'The Social Function of Greek Tragedy', and S. Goldhill, 'Civic Ideology and the Problem of Difference: the Politics of Aeschylean Tragedy, once again', *Journal of Hellenic Studies*, vol. 120, 2000. On issues of gender and power, see H. Foley, *Female Acts in Greek Tragedy* (Princeton, 2001); V. Wohl, *Intimate Commerce: Exchange, Gender and Subjectivity in Greek Tragedy* (Austin, TX, 1998). On music and metre, see W. Scott, *Musical Design in Aeschylean Theater* (Hanover, NH, 1982). For general discussion of tragedy, see M. Silk, ed., *Tragedy and the Tragic: Greek Theatre and Beyond* (Oxford, 1996), and, especially, P. Easterling, ed., *The Cambridge Companion to Greek Tragedy* (Cambridge, 1997). On the material and social conditions of the theatre, see E. Csapo and W. Slater, *The Context of Ancient Drama* (Ann Arbor, 1995); D. Wiles, *Tragedy in Athens: Performance Space and Theatrical Meaning* (Cambridge, 1997), and P. Wilson, *The Athenian Institution of the Khoregia: the Chorus, the City and the Stage* (Cambridge, 2000). For other works, see the bibliographies on individual chapters below.

1 Drama and the city of Athens

J. Davies, *Democracy and Classical Greece* (Hassocks, 1978); P. Easterling and J. Muir, edd., *Greek Religion and Society* (Cambridge, 1985); M. Finley, *Politics in the Ancient World* (Cambridge, 1983); W. G. Forrest, *The Emergence of Greek Democracy* (London, 1966); S. Goldhill, *Reading Greek Tragedy* (Cambridge, 1986); S. Goldhill, 'The Great Dionysia and Civic Ideology', in J. Winkler and F. Zeitlin, edd., *Nothing to do with Dionysus?* (Princeton, 1990); R. Gordon, ed., *Myth, Religion and Society* (Cambridge, 1981); M. Hansen, *The Athenian Democracy in the Age of Demosthenes* (Oxford, 1991); J. Henderson, 'Women and the Athenian Dramatic Festivals', in *Transactions and Proceedings of the American Philological Association*, vol. 121, 1991; G. E. R. Lloyd, *The Revolutions of Wisdom* (Berkeley, 1987); N. Loraux, *The Invention of Athens* (Cambridge, Mass., 1986); P. B. Manville, *The Origins of Citizenship in Ancient Athens* (Princeton, 1990); J. Ober, *Mass and Elite in Democratic Athens* (Princeton, 1989); R. Osborne, *Classical Landscape with Figures* (London, 1987); R. Sinclair, *Democracy and Participation in Athens* (Cambridge, 1988); O. Taplin, *The Stagecraft of Aeschylus* (Oxford, 1977); W. Tyrrell, *Amazons: a Study in Athenian Mythmaking* (Baltimore, 1984); J.-P. Vernant, *Myth and Society in Ancient Greece* (London, 1980); *Myth and Thought among the Greeks* (London, 1983); J.-P. Vernant and P. Vidal-Naquet,

Myth and Tragedy in Ancient Greece (Cambridge, Mass., 1990), 2 vols. in one paperback; P. Vidal-Naquet, *The Black Hunter* (Baltimore, 1986).

2 *The* Oresteia

M. Arthur, 'Early Greece: the Origins of Western Attitudes towards Women', *Arethusa*, vol. 6, 1973 (reprinted in *Women in the Ancient World*, edd. J. Peradotto and J. P. Sullivan (Albany, 1984)); J. Bamberger, 'The Myth of Matriarchy', in M. Rosaldo and L. Lamphere, edd., *Women, Culture and Society* (Stanford, 1975); A. Brown, 'The Erinyes in the *Oresteia*, Real Life, the Supernatural and the Stage', *Journal of Hellenic Studies*, vol. 103, 1983; W. Burkert, *Homo Neceans* (Berkeley, 1983); D. Clay, 'Aeschylus' Trigeron Mythos', *Hermes*, vol. 97, 1969; M. Detienne and J.-P. Vernant, *The Cuisine of Sacrifice* (Chicago, 1988); E. Dodds, 'Morals and Politics in the *Oresteia*', *Proceedings of the Cambridge Philological Society*, vol. 6, 1960; K. Dover, 'The Political Aspect of Aeschylus' *Eumenides*', *Journal of Hellenic Studies*, vol. 77, 1957; H. Foley, 'The "Female Intruder" Reconsidered', *Classical Philology*, vol. 77, 1982; R. Girard, *Violence and the Sacred* (Baltimore, 1977); *S. Goldhill, *Language, Sexuality, Narrative: the Oresteia* (Cambridge, 1984); S. Goldhill, *Reading Greek Tragedy* (Cambridge, 1986); J. Gould, 'Law, Custom, Myth: Aspects of the Social Position of Women in Classical Athens', *Journal of Hellenic Studies*, vol. 100, 1980; J. Gould, 'Homeric Epic and the Tragic Moment', in *Aspects of the Epic*, edd. T. Winnifrith, P. Murray and K. Gransden (London, 1983); J. Jones, *On Aristotle and Greek Tragedy* (London, 1962); H. Kitto, *Greek Tragedy* (London, 1961); B. Knox, 'The Lion in the House', *Classical Philology*, vol. 47, 1952 (reprinted in B. Knox, *Word and Action* (Baltimore, 1979)); *A. Lebeck, *The Oresteia* (Washington, 1971); C. Macleod, 'Politics and the *Oresteia*', *Journal of Hellenic Studies*, vol. 102, 1982; C. Meier, *The Greek Discovery of Politics* (Cambridge, Mass., 1990); G. Nagy, *Pindar's Homer* (Baltimore, 1990); M. Nussbaum, *The Fragility of Goodness* (Cambridge, 1986); T. Tanner, *Adultery and the Novel* (Baltimore, 1980); J.-P. Vernant and P. Vidal-Naquet, *Myth and Tragedy in Ancient Greece* (Cambridge, Mass., 1990), 2 vols. in one paperback; P. Vidal-Naquet, *The Black Hunter* (Baltimore, 1986); R. Winnington-Ingram, *Studies in Aeschylus* (Cambridge, 1983); *F. Zeitlin, 'The Motif of the Corrupted Sacrifice in Aeschylus' *Oresteia*', *Transactions and Proceedings of the American Philological Association*, vol. 96, 1965; F. Zeitlin, 'Dynamics of Misogyny in the *Oresteia*', *Arethusa* 11, 1978 (reprinted in her fine collection of essays *Playing the Other* (Chicago, 1996)).

3 The influence of the Oresteia

J. Bachofen, *Myth, Religion and Mother Right: Selected Writings* (London, 1967); H. Cixous, 'Sorties', in H. Cixous and C. Clement, *The Newly Born Woman* (Minneapolis, 1986); B. Knox, *The Heroic Temper* (Berkeley, 1964); K. Millet, *Sexual Politics* (New York, 1971); C. Segal, *Tragedy and Civilization* (Cambridge, Mass., 1981); M. S. Silk and J. P. Stern, *Nietzsche on Tragedy* (Cambridge, 1981); R. Winnington-Ingram, *Sophocles: an Interpretation* (Cambridge, 1980).